THE RAINBOW METHOD

A Colorful Introduction to Staff Reading and Piano Playing

PRIMER LEVEL

Dr. Ariel Nathanson Bolinja

Artwork by Anna Sziabowski

ISBN: 979-8-218-77537-7

Table of Contents

THE NOTES OF THE TREBLE CLEF

THE NOTES OF THE BASS CLEF

SHARPS AND FLATS • TREBLE A AND B

GRADUATION

INTRODUCTION TO THE PIANO

Posture and Hand Shape

Rounded Hand Shape

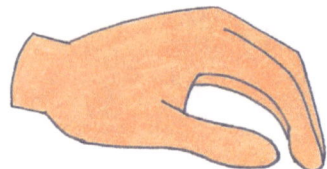 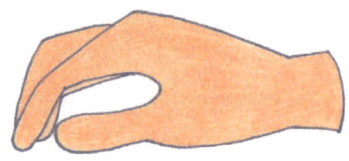

We play piano with a rounded hand shape so that all of our fingers can easily play the keys.

Hand Shape Activity:

1. Place your hand flat on the piano. Did you notice how all of your fingers are different lengths? Some fingers can't reach the keys when we play with a flat hand.

2. Now place your hand in a rounded position on the piano. Now each finger can easily play the keys!

Posture

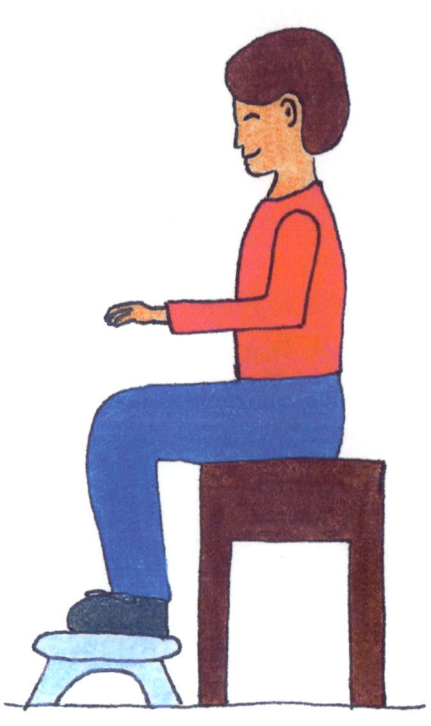

Sit up tall and support your arms like the image above. Make sure your feet are resting on a footstool or flat on the floor.

Finger Numbers

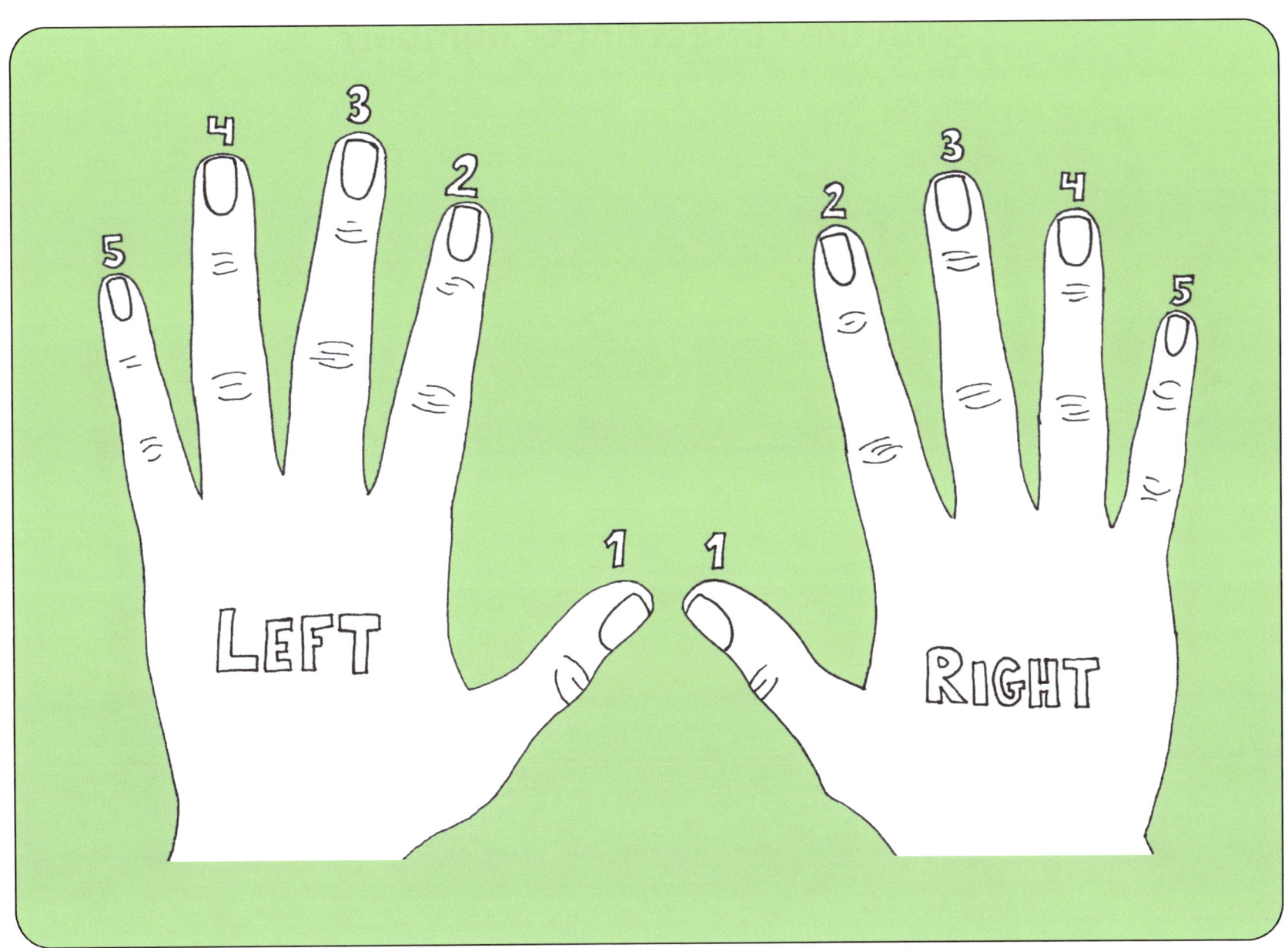

**Can you label each finger
with the correct finger number?**

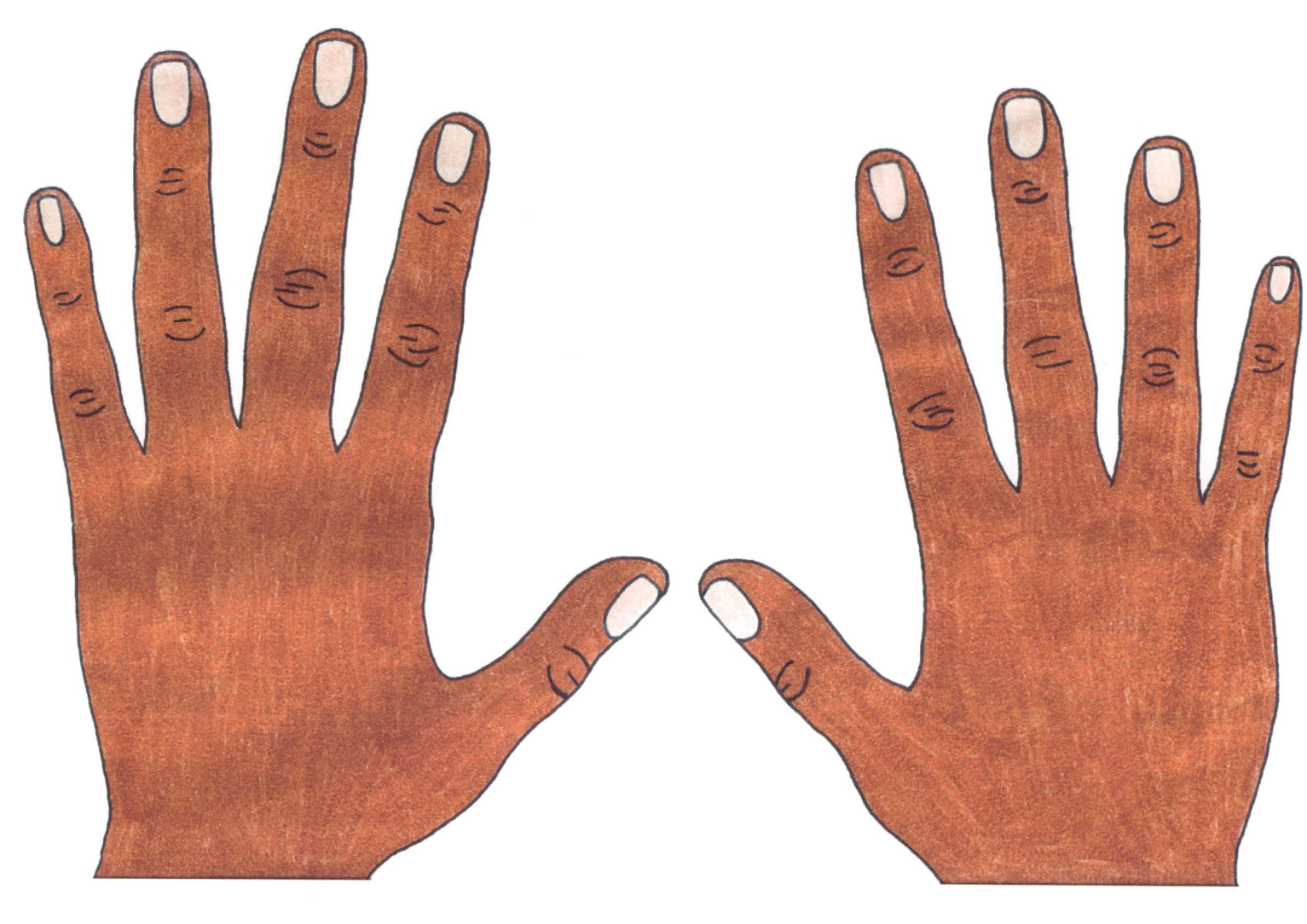

Right Hand and Left Hand Fun!

1. Write RH inside each right hand and write LH inside each left hand.

2. Color each right hand blue and each left hand green.

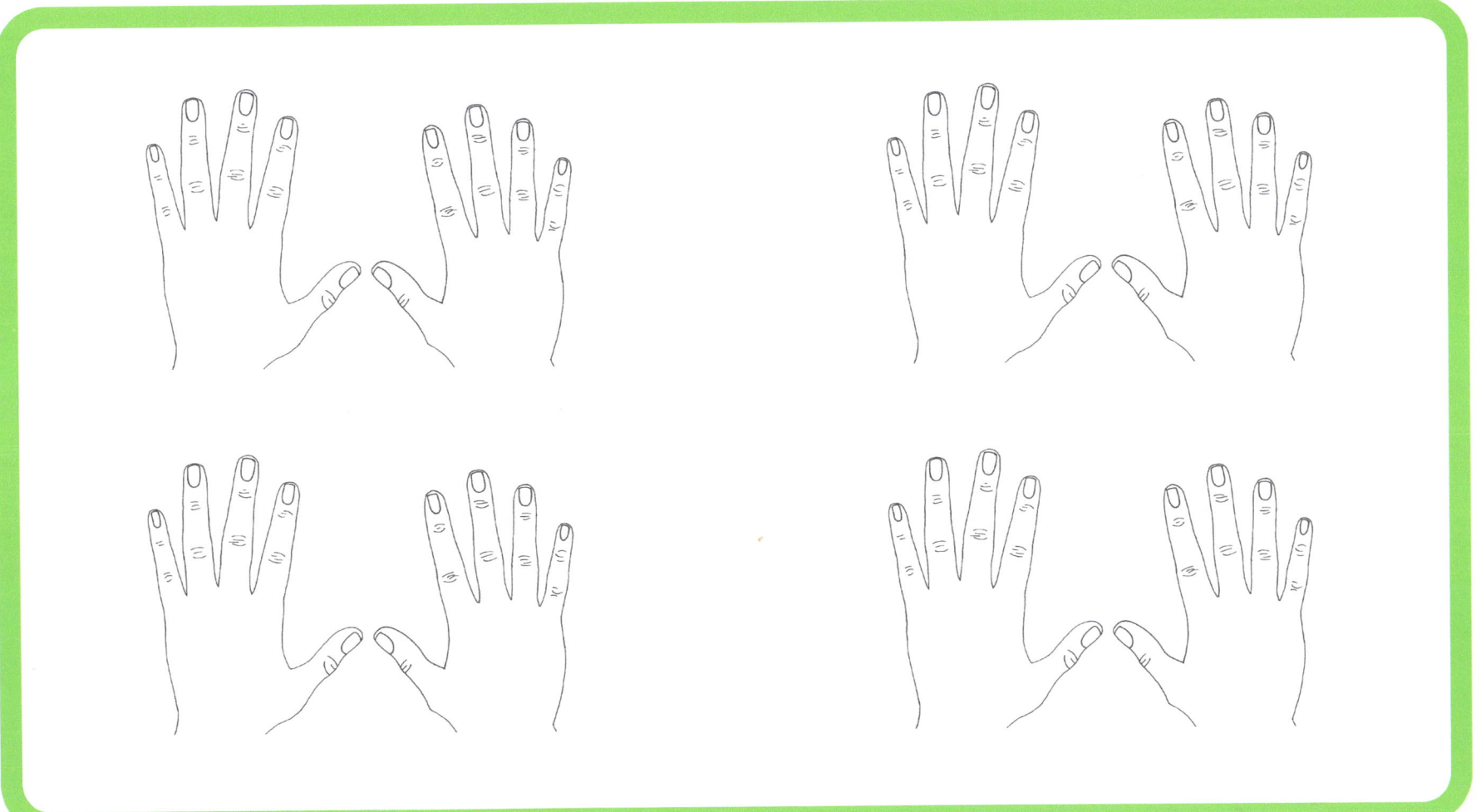

High Notes and Low Notes on the Piano

Low   **High**

Moving Lower   **Moving Higher**

Activity Corner:

1. Your teacher will demonstrate notes moving higher and notes moving lower on the piano.

2. Can you show your teacher how to play notes moving higher and notes moving lower?

THE BLACK KEYS

Groups of Black Keys

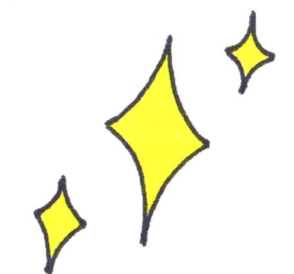

On the piano, there are groups of two black keys and groups of three black keys.

Groups of Two   **Groups of Three**

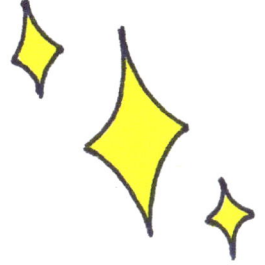

Activity Corner:

1. Can you count the groups of black keys?
2. How many groups of two black keys are there?
3. How many groups of three black keys are there?

Black Key Safari

Circle the groups of three black keys in green.

Circle the groups of two black keys in blue.

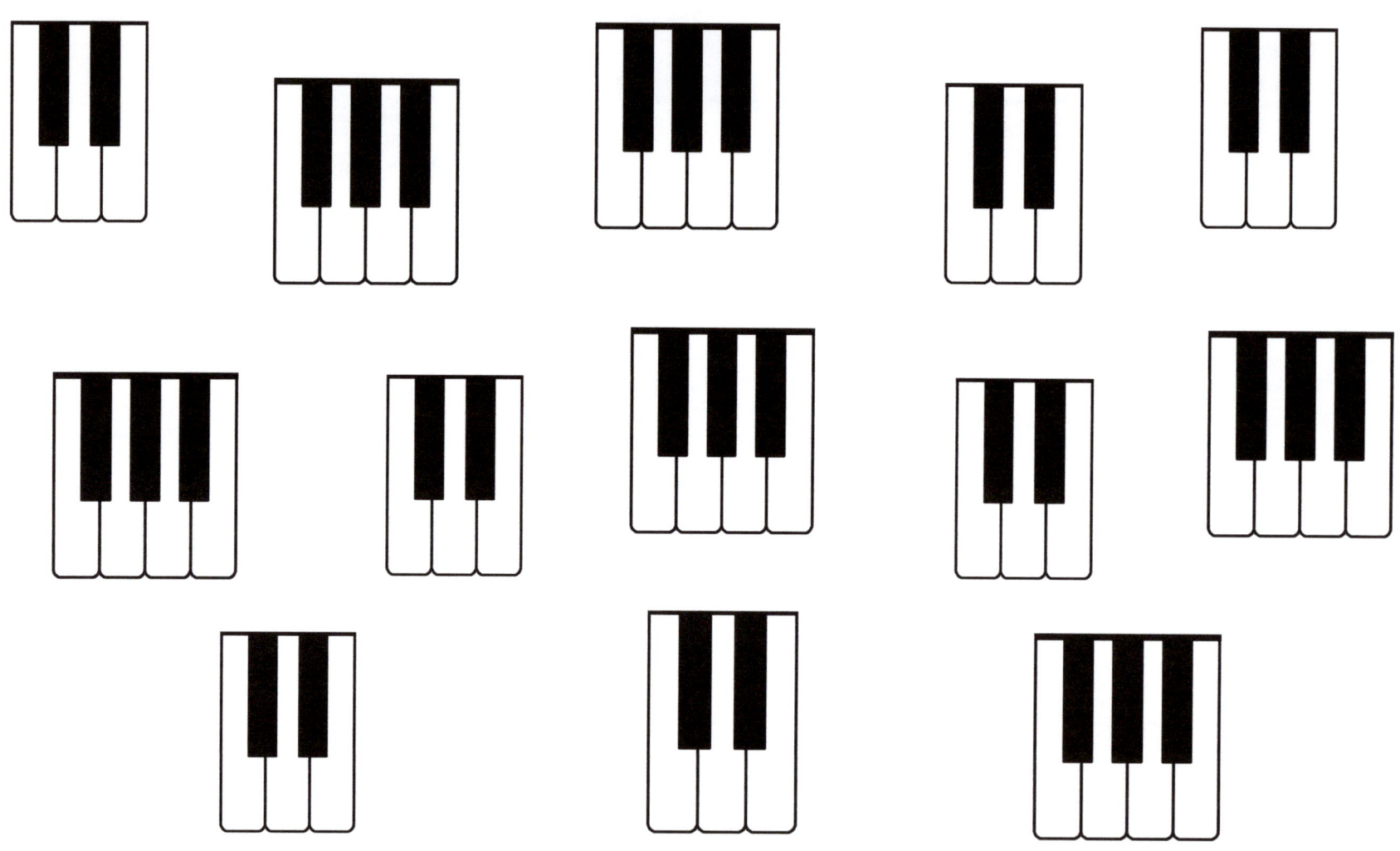

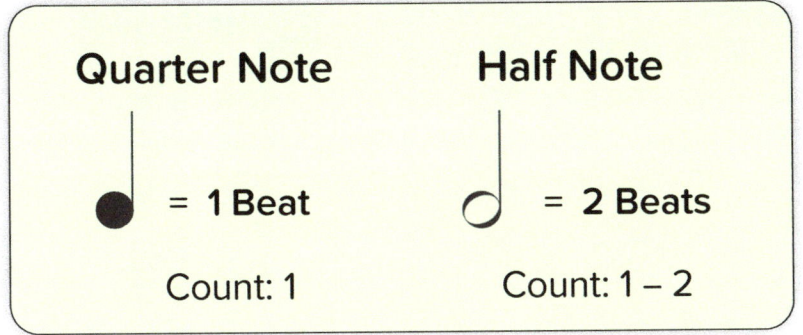

Quarter Note

♩ = 1 Beat

Count: 1

Half Note

�half = 2 Beats

Count: 1 – 2

Right Hand

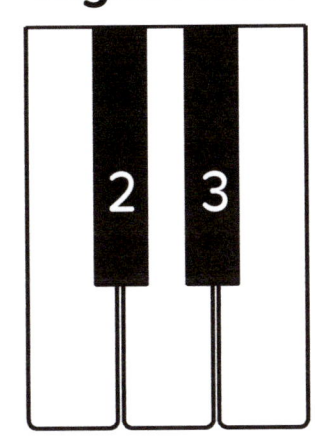

Play this piece on any group of two black keys on the piano.

Walking in the Garden

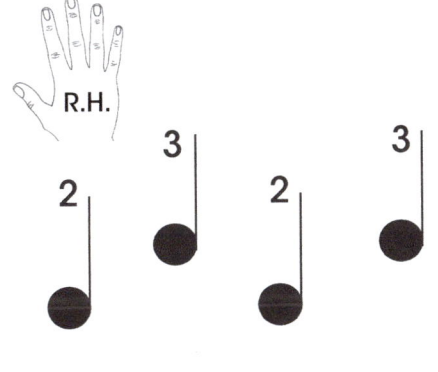

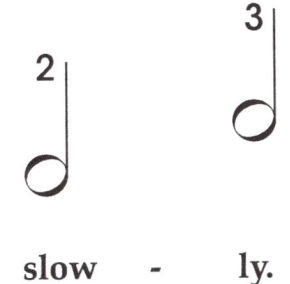

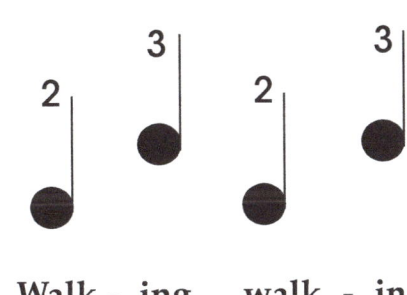

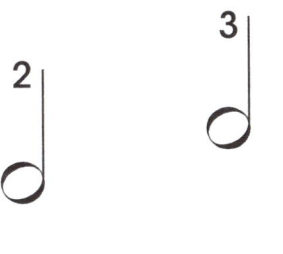

Walk - ing, walk - ing   slow - ly.   Walk - ing, walk - ing,   slow - ly.

11

Dynamics tell us the volume of the notes we play. In this piece, we use two different dynamics.

f (forte) = loud

p (piano) = soft

Right Hand

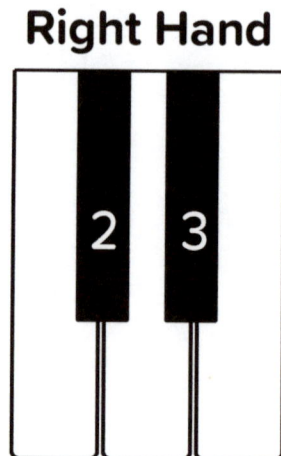

Birds in the Sky

Move up to the next highest group of two black keys each time the notes move up.

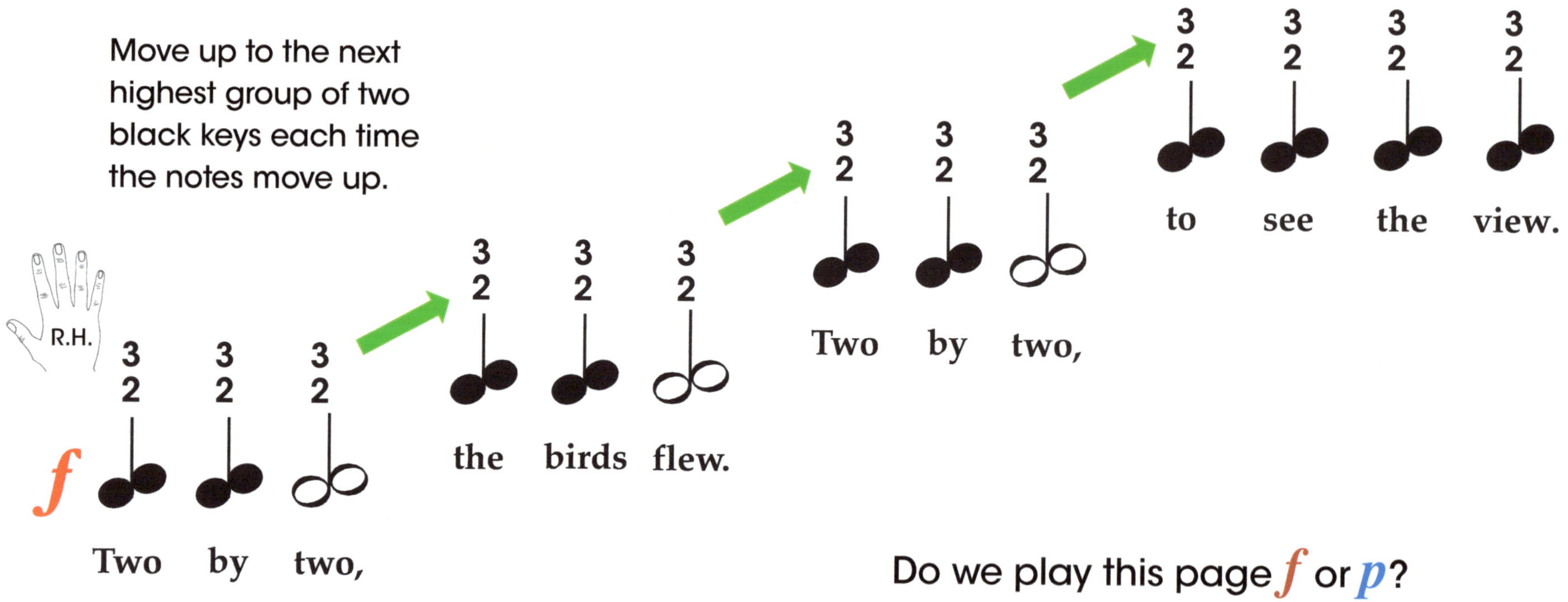

R.H.

f

Two   by   two,

the   birds   flew.

Two   by   two,

to   see   the   view.

Do we play this page *f* or *p*?

Move down to the next
lowest group of two
black keys each time the
notes move down.

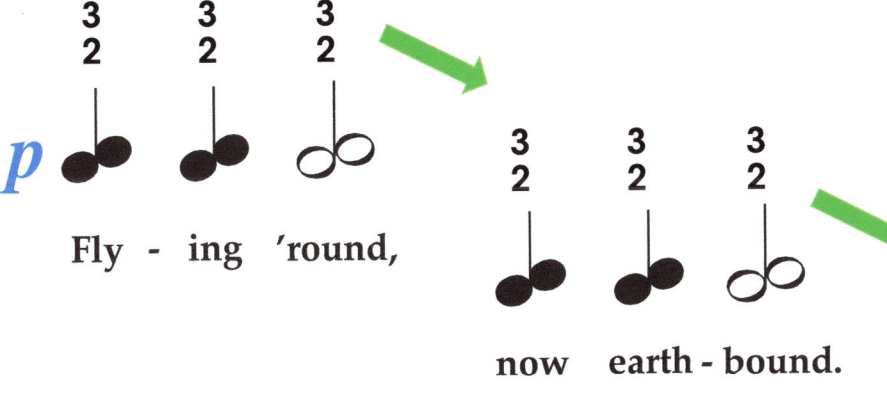

Fly - ing 'round,

now earth - bound.

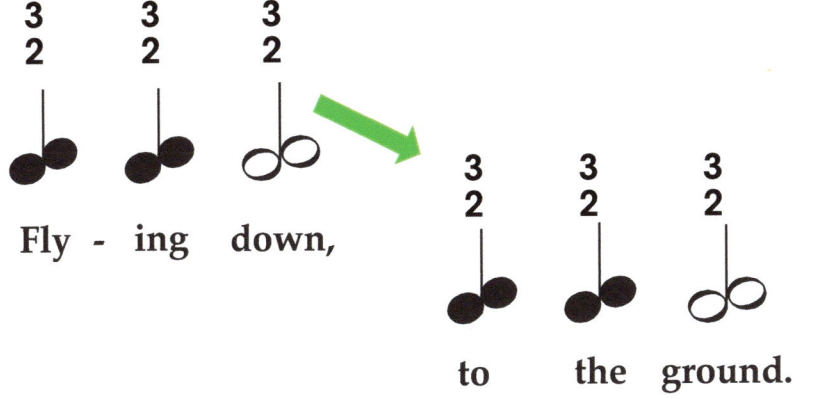

Fly - ing down,

to the ground.

Do we play this page *f* or *p*?

Bar Line

Bar lines divide the music into small groups of notes called measures to make it easier for us to count.

Can you count how many measures there are in this piece?

Left hand **Right hand**

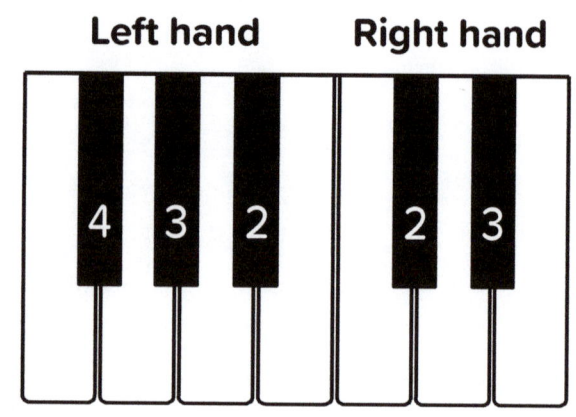

Groups of Two and Three Black Keys

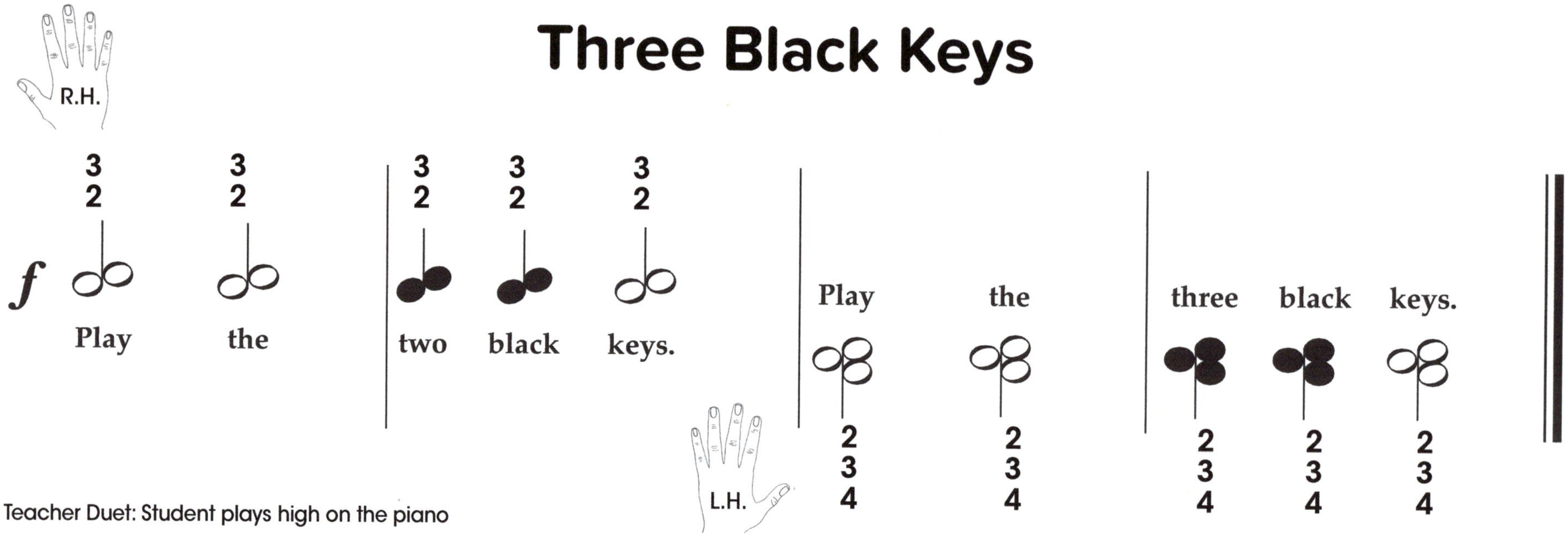

R.H.

f

3 / 2 — Play

3 / 2 — the

3 / 2 two **3 / 2** black **3 / 2** keys.

Play — **2 3 4**

the — **2 3 4**

L.H.

three — **2 3 4** black — **2 3 4** keys. — **2 3 4**

Teacher Duet: Student plays high on the piano

R.H. 1

L.H. 5   1

L.H. 5   1   4   2

14

Repeat Sign

Repeat from the beginning.

Dotted Half Note

$\dot{\jmath} \cdot$ = 3 Beats

Count: 1 - 2 - 3

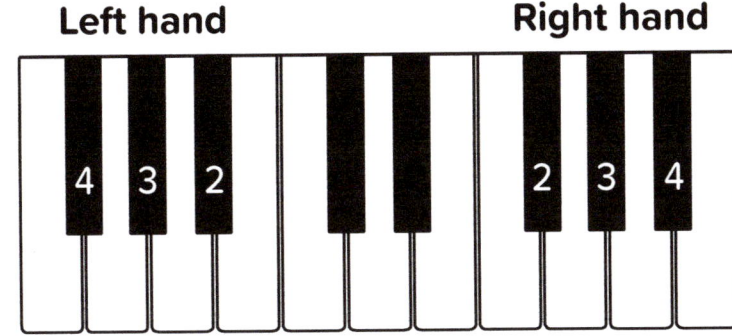

Left hand   Right hand

The Mime

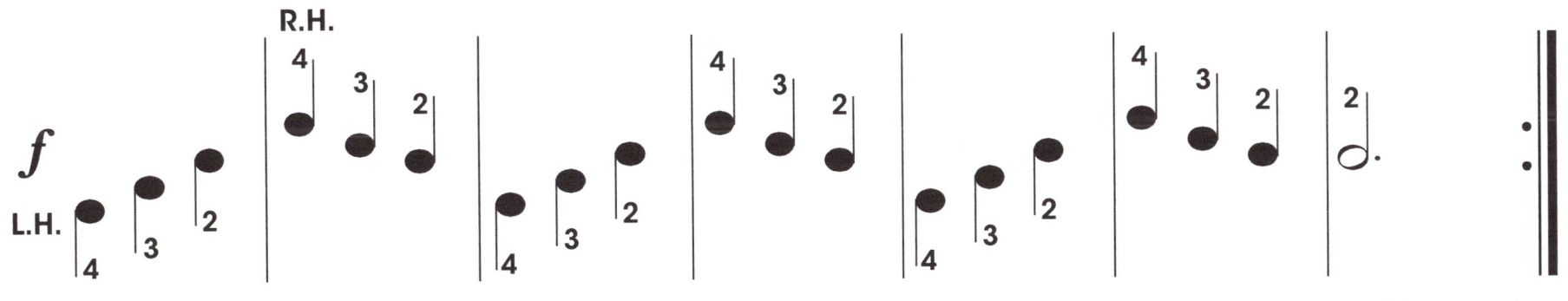

4,   3,   2,   4,   3,   2.   Step - ping up,   step - ping down. Left hand plays, right hand plays. Hold,   2,   3!

Teacher Duet: Student plays high on the piano

Whole Note

𝅝 = 4 Beats

Count: 1 - 2 - 3 - 4

Left hand   Right hand

Stargazer

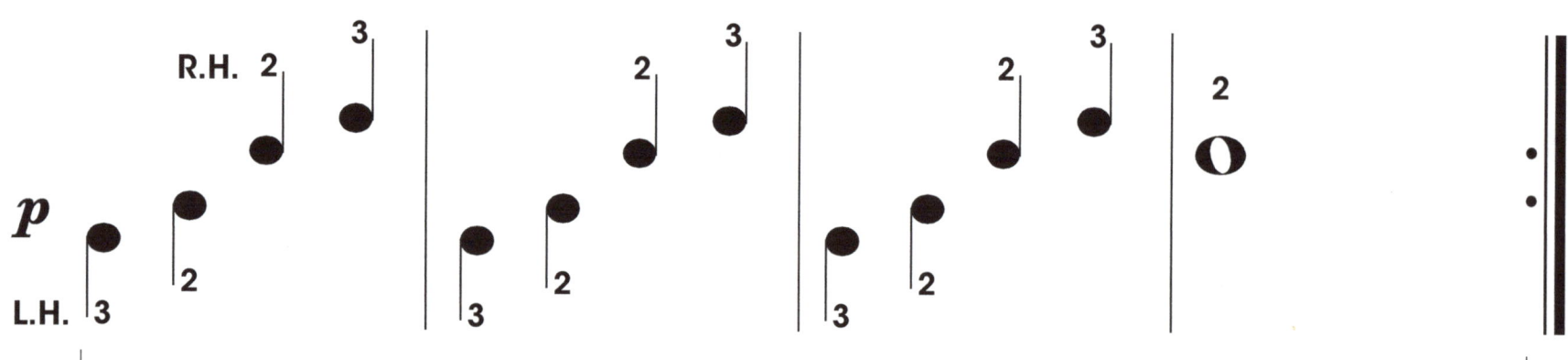

Damper Pedal Marking

The damper pedal is the pedal on the right side.

Put pedal down   Pick pedal up

Composition Corner:

Can you create your own composition using the black keys and the pedal?

THE WHITE KEYS

The White Keys and the Musical Alphabet

The musical alphabet has 7 notes.

A B C D E F G

The piano has 88 keys. The lowest note on the piano is A.
The highest note on the piano is C.

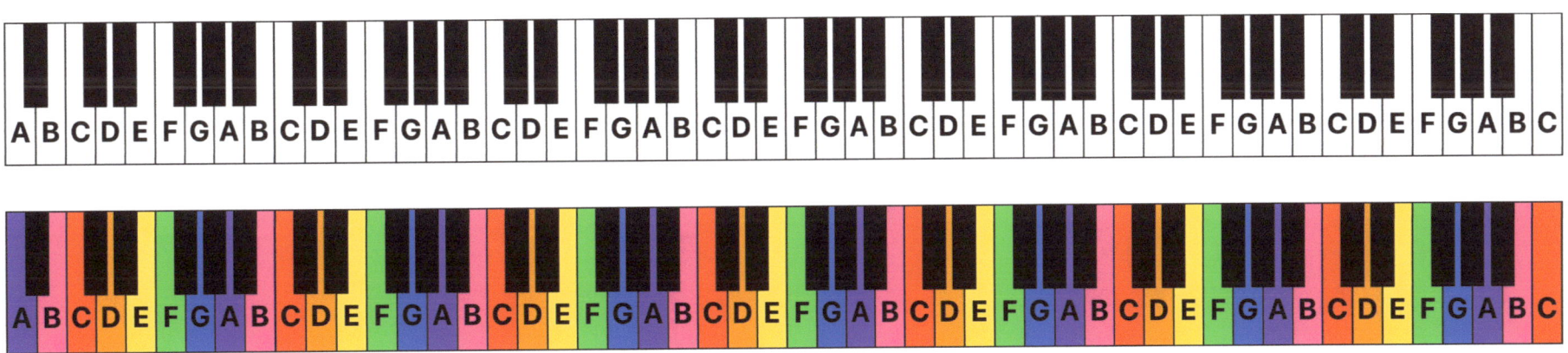

Learning C, D, E

C is to the left of a group of two black keys.

D is in between a group of two black keys.

E is to the right of a group of two black keys.

Circle the groups of C, D, E on the keyboard below.

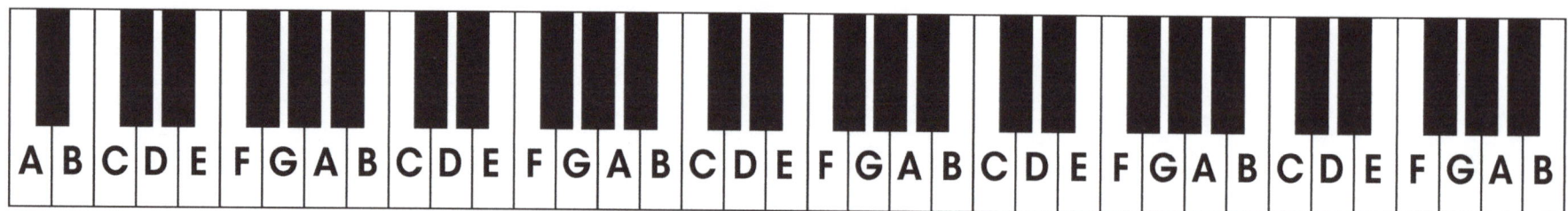

A B C D E F G A B C D E F G A B C D E F G A B C D E F G A B C D E F G A B C D E F G A B

Write the names of the colored notes in the boxes below.

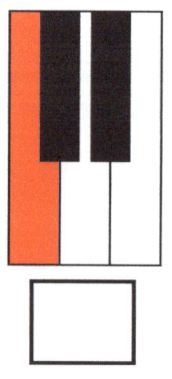
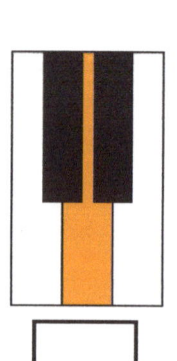
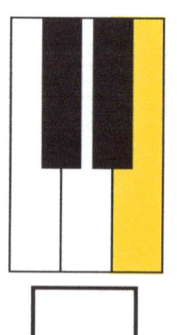
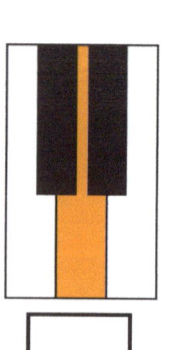
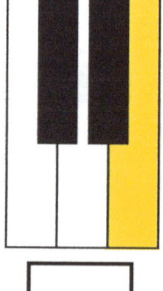
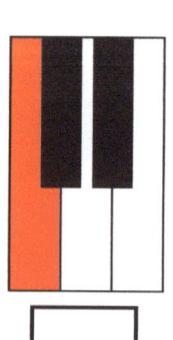

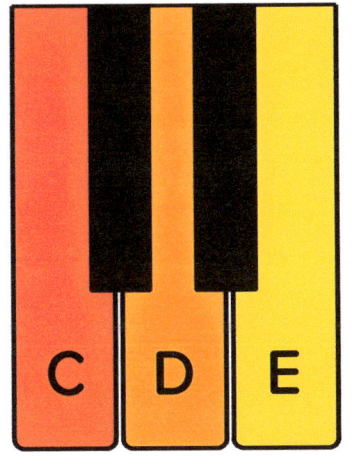

Place your right hand on C, D, E in the middle of the piano.

C, D, E

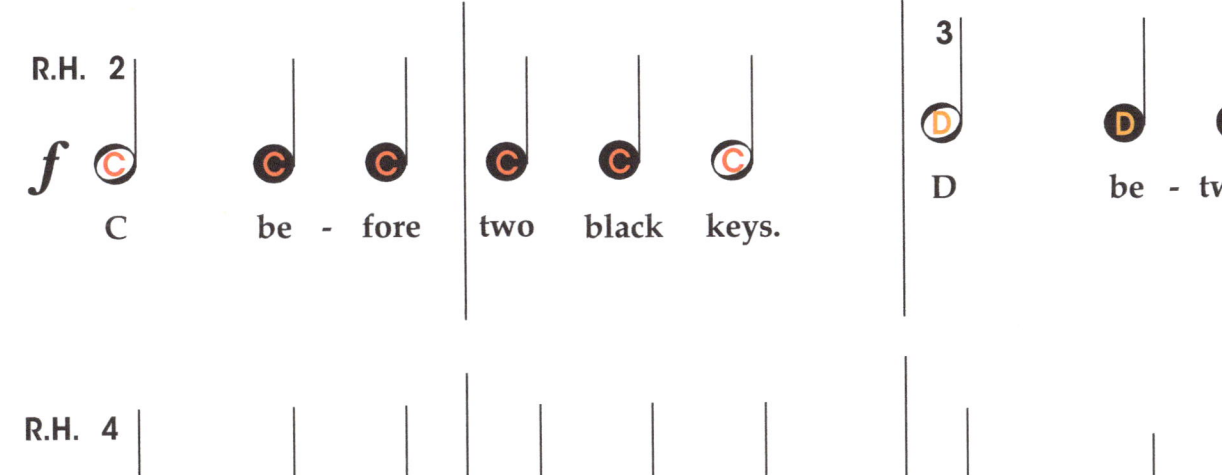

R.H. 2

𝑓 C C C C C C
C be - fore two black keys.

3 D D D D D D
D be - tween two black keys.

R.H. 4

E E E E E E
E af - ter two black keys.

E, D,

2 C
C!

Learning F, G, A, B

F is to the left of a group of three black keys.

G comes after F.

A comes after G.

B is to the right of a group of three black keys.

Circle the groups of F, G, A, B on the keyboard below.

C D E F G A B C D E F G A B C D E F G A B C D E F G A B C D E F G A B C D E F G A B

Write the names of the colored notes in the boxes below.

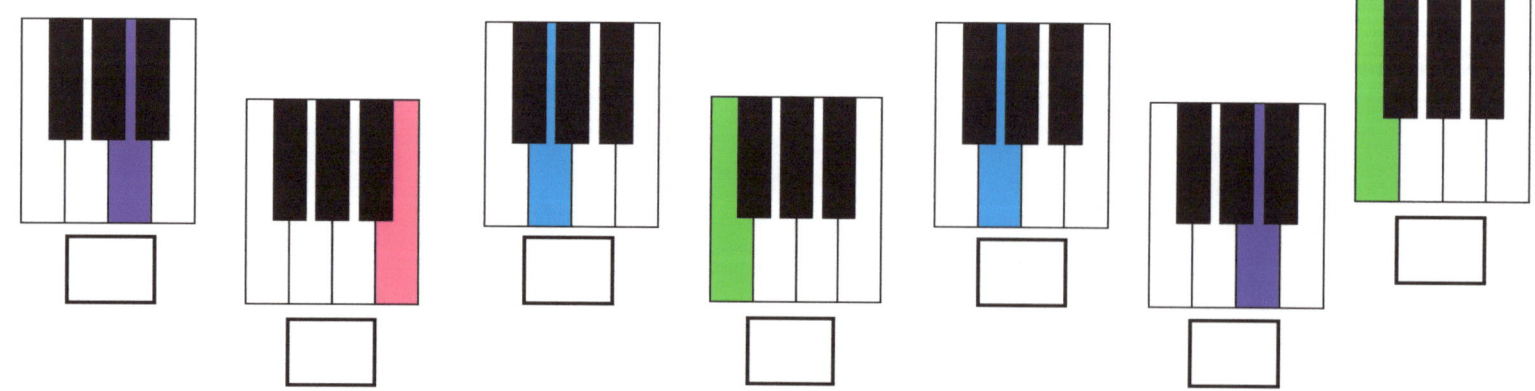

20

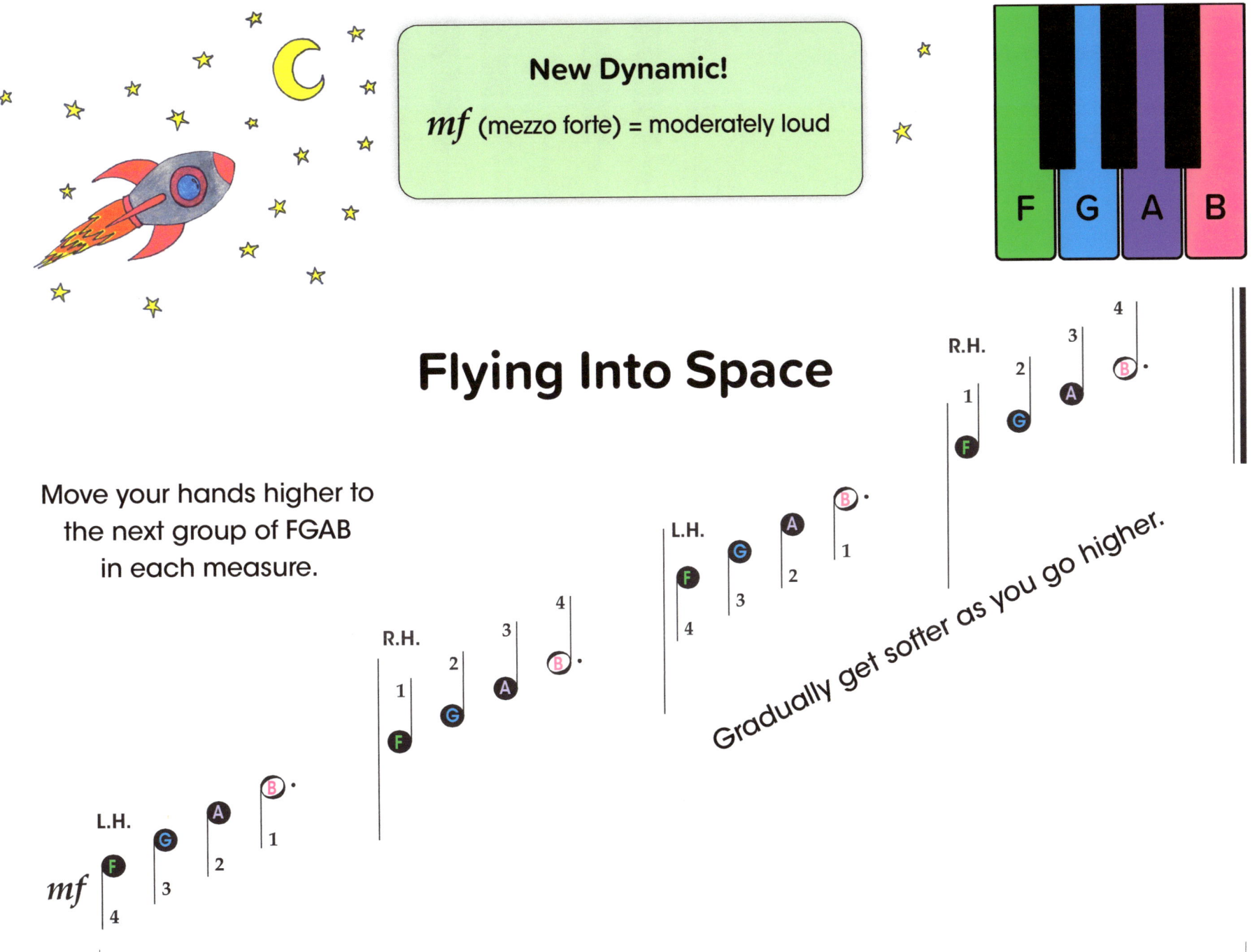

New Dynamic!

mf (mezzo forte) = moderately loud

Flying Into Space

Move your hands higher to the next group of FGAB in each measure.

Gradually get softer as you go higher.

Performance Tip

Gradually play louder to make it seem like the shark is swimming closer and closer!

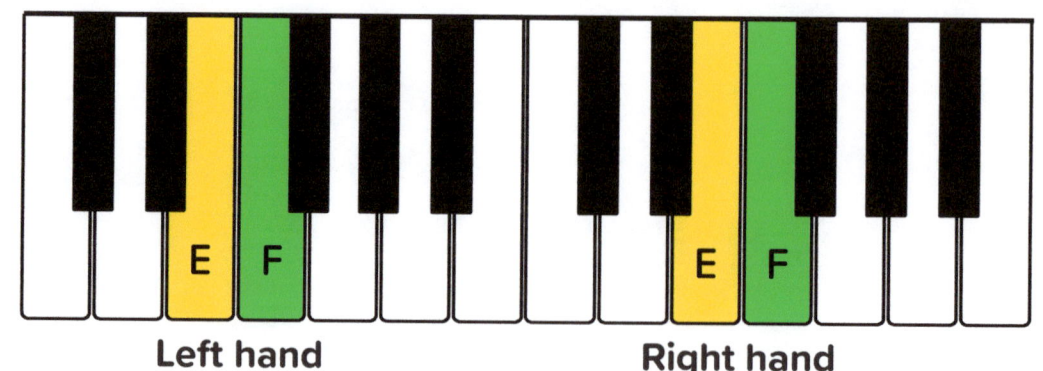

Sharks

Play low on the piano.

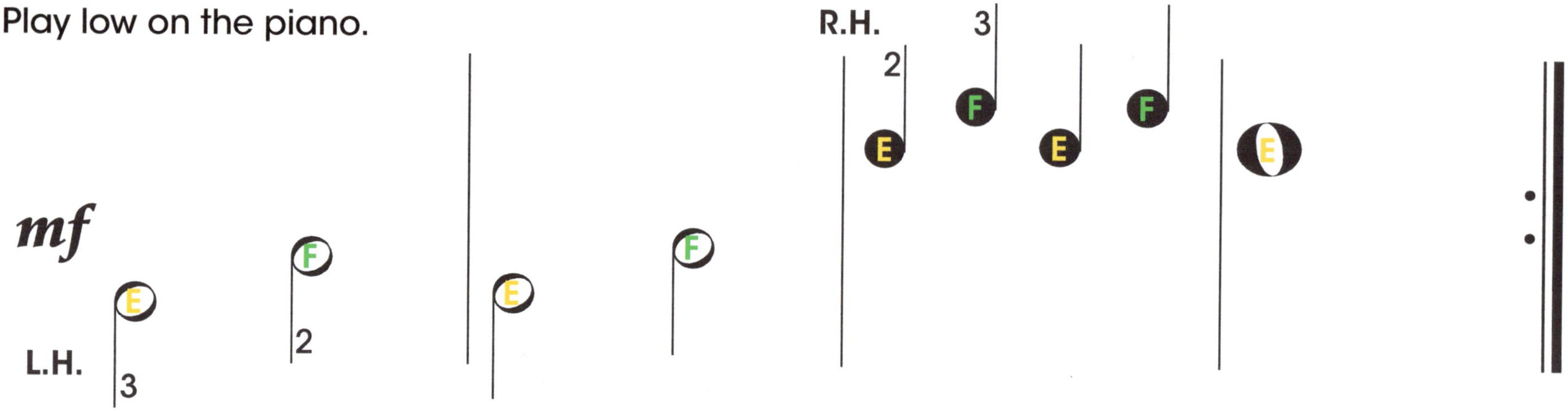

mf

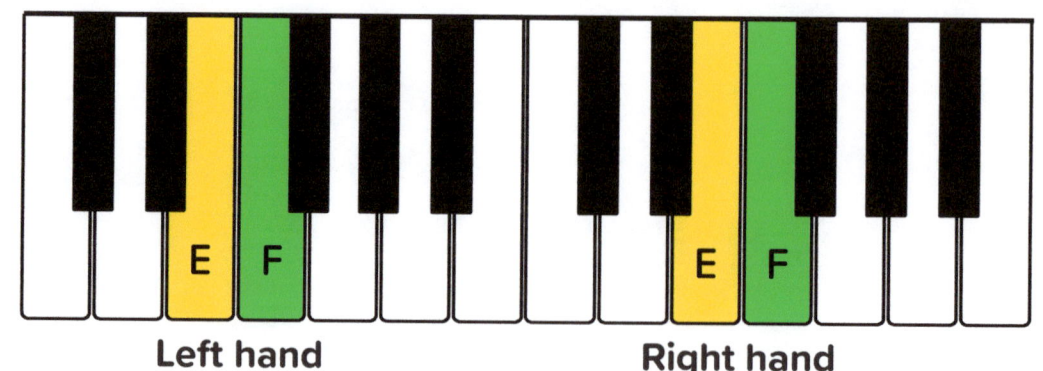

22

Activity Corner:

Draw a picture of dinosaur footsteps in the space below.

C
G

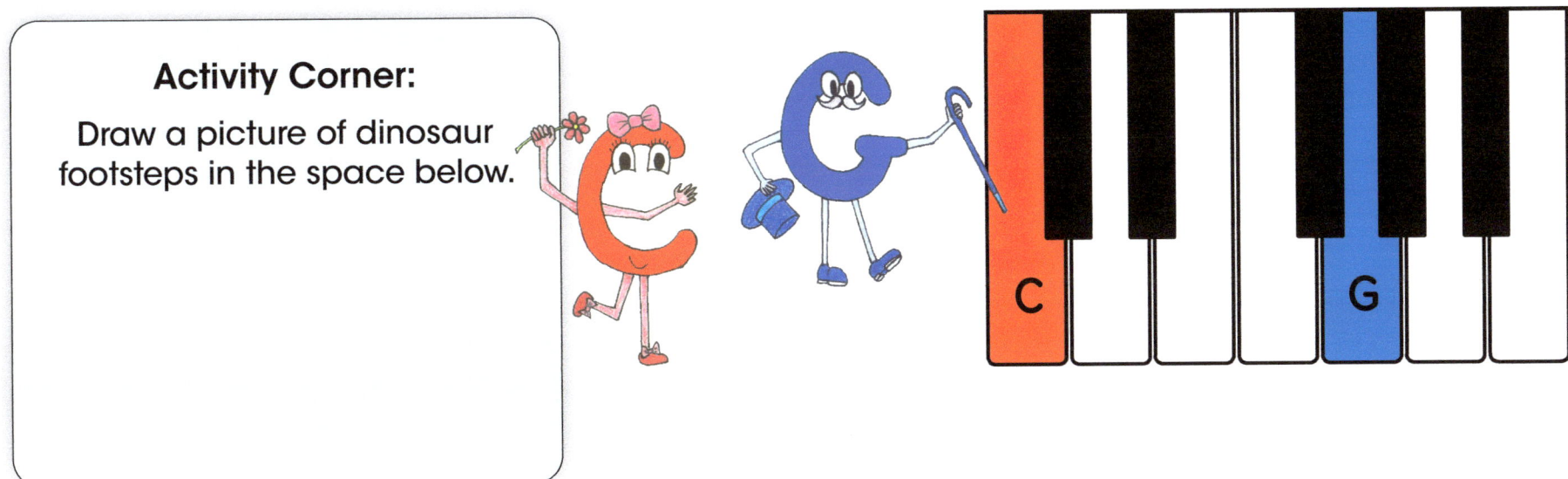

Dinosaur Footsteps

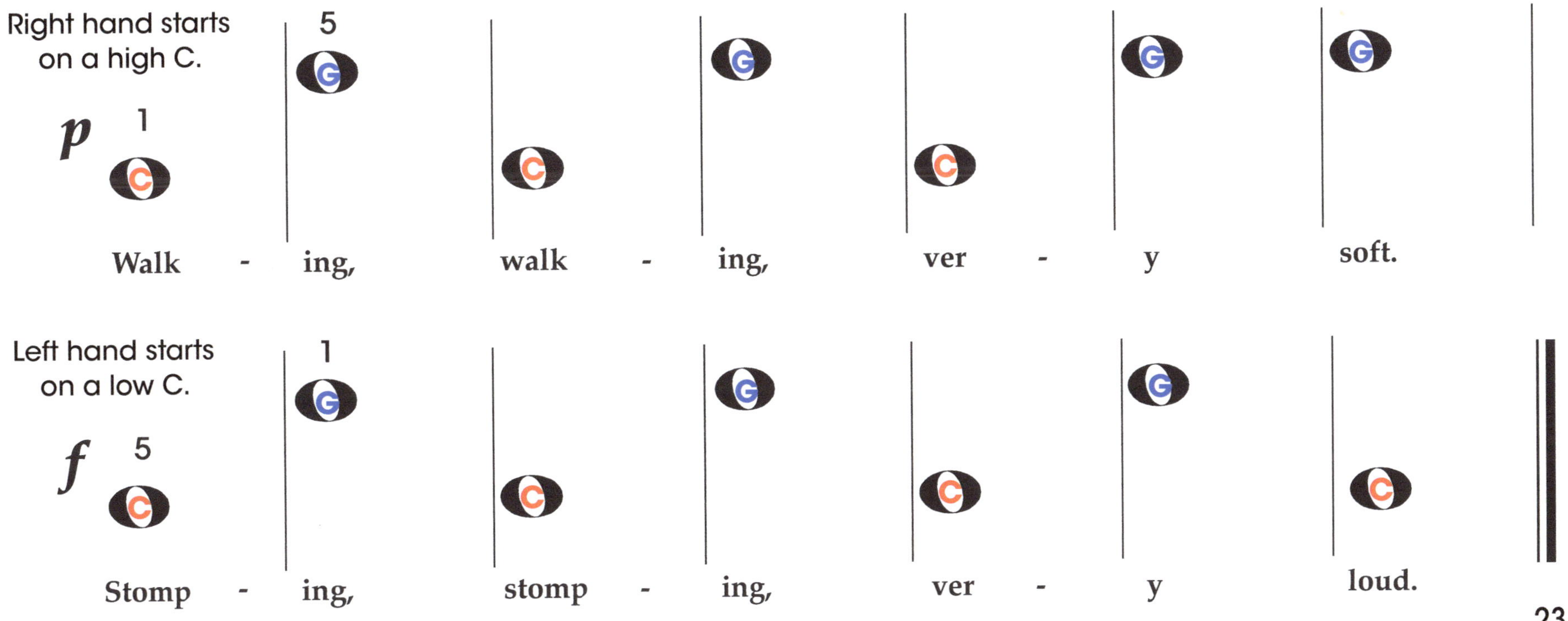
Right hand starts on a high C.
p
1
5
Walk - ing, walk - ing, ver - y soft.
Left hand starts on a low C.
f
5
1
Stomp - ing, stomp - ing, ver - y loud.

Time Signatures

The time signature is two numbers at the beginning of the piece that tell us how to count the music.

4 = Count 1-2-3-4

4 = ♩ gets 1 beat

4 The top number tells us the number of beats that are in each measure. In this case, there are 4 beats!

4 The bottom number tells us the type of note that gets 1 beat. In this case, quarter notes get 1 beat!

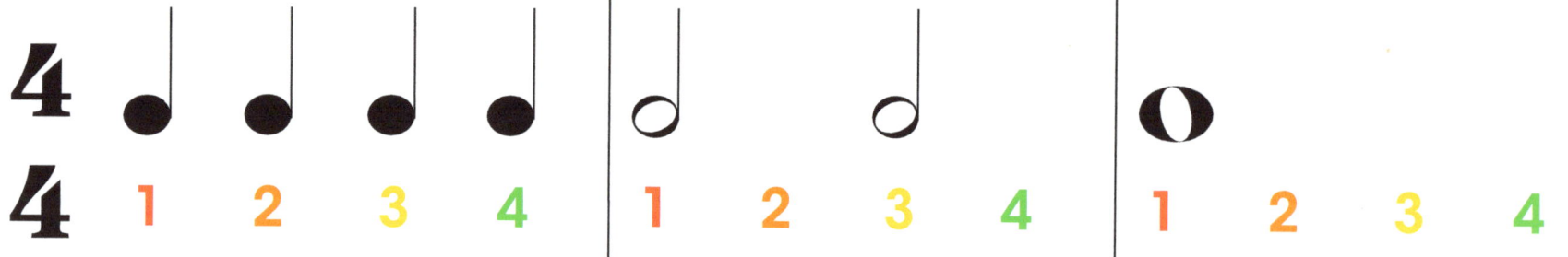

Activity Corner:

1. Can you count and clap the rhythm above?
2. Pick a note on the piano. Play the rhythm above on the note you picked, and count out loud.

Activity Corner:

1. Count the number of measures in this piece.
2. Count and clap the rhythm.

Look at the time signature at the beginning of the piece. How do you need to count in each measure?

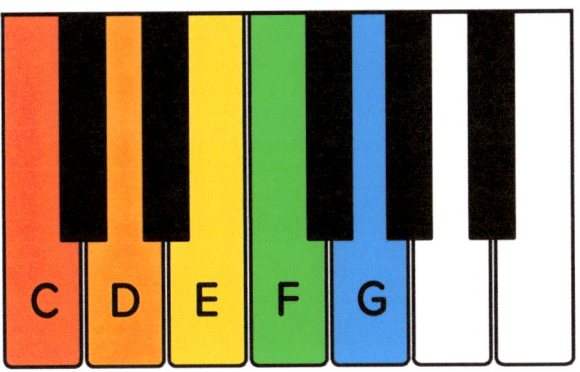

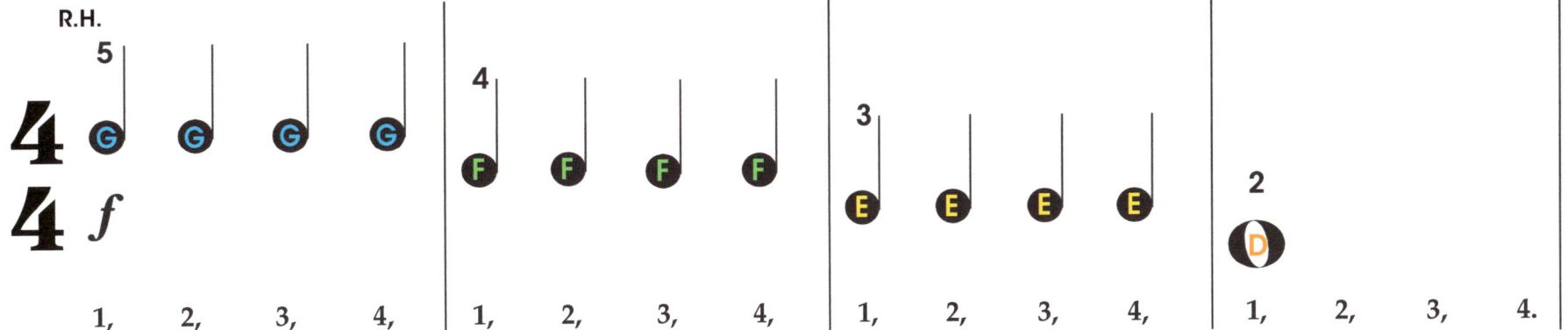

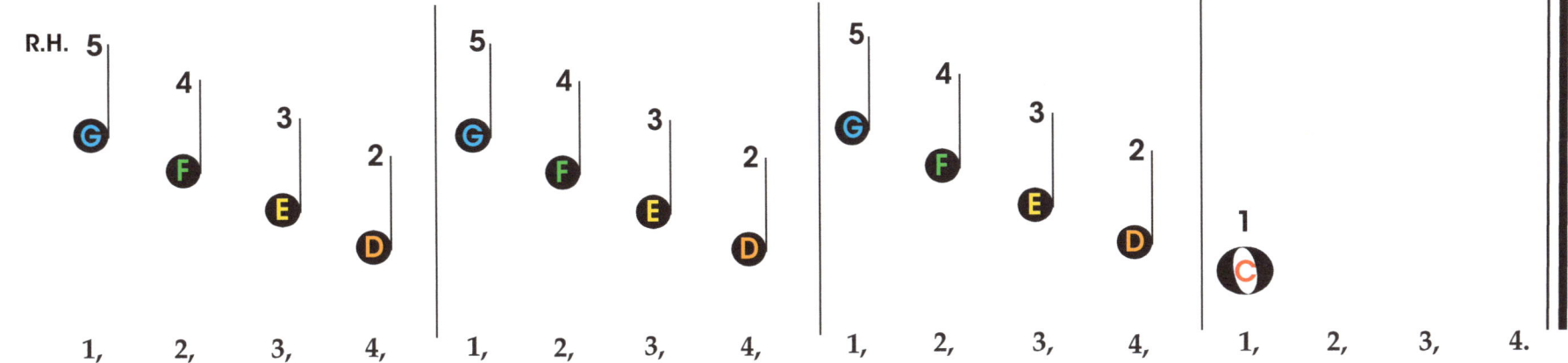

Write the musical alphabet in the spaces below.

___ ___ ___ ___ ___ ___ ___

Write the musical alphabet backwards in the spaces below.

___ ___ ___ ___ ___ ___ ___

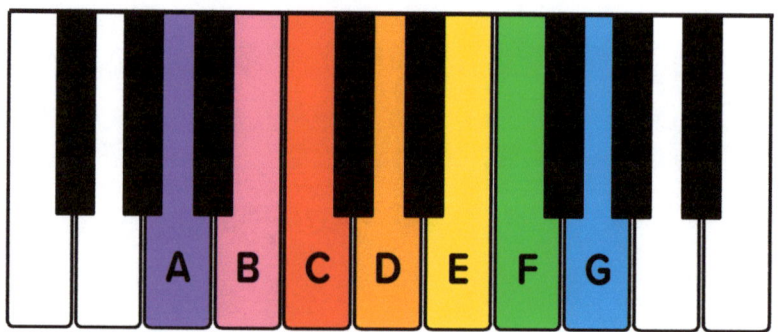

The Musical Alphabet Song

Play this piece in the middle section of the piano.

26

White Key Safari

Write the names of the colored
notes in the boxes below.

THE STAFF

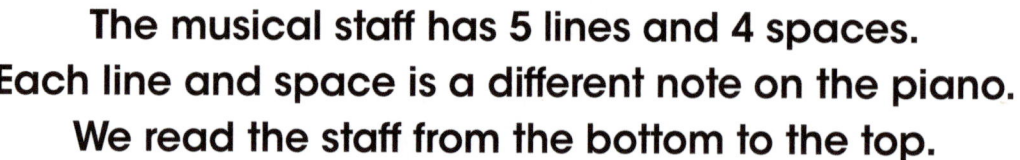

The musical staff has 5 lines and 4 spaces.
Each line and space is a different note on the piano.
We read the staff from the bottom to the top.

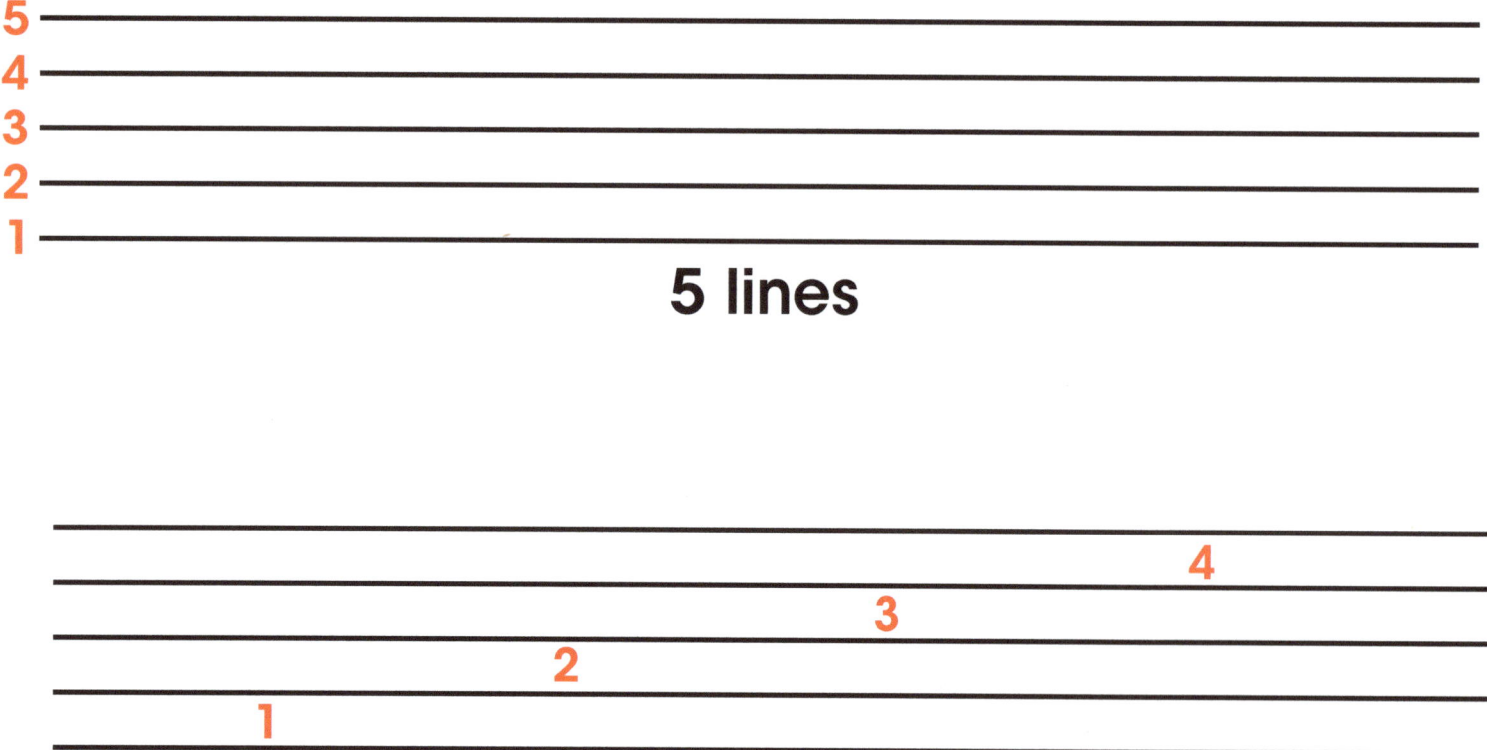

5 lines

4 spaces

Line Notes and Space Notes

Line Notes

Line notes have the staff line going through their center.

Space Notes

Space notes are on the spaces between the staff lines.

Line Note

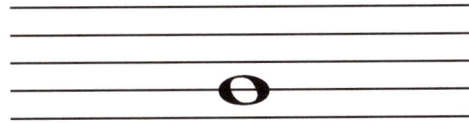

Space Note

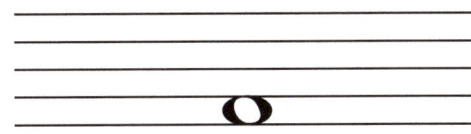

Activity Corner: Write **L** underneath the line notes and **S** underneath the space notes.

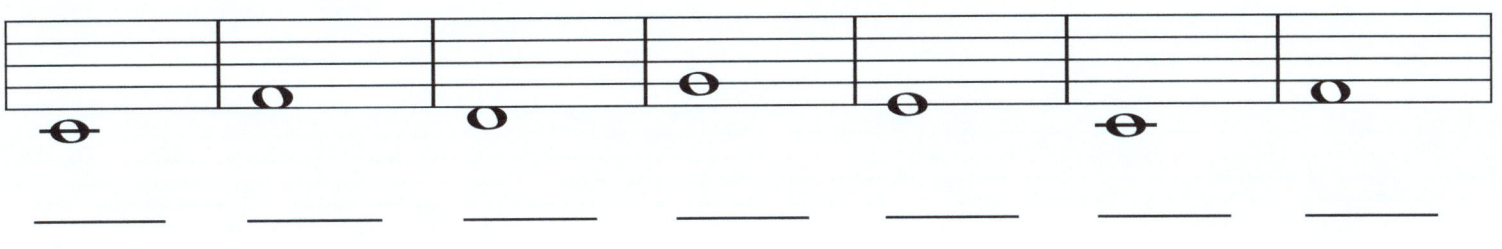

The Grand Staff

Piano music has two staves.
The top staff is for the right hand because our right hand is closest to the high notes. The bottom staff is for the left hand because our left hand is closest to the low notes.

Treble Clef

The high notes
on the piano

Bass Clef

The low notes
on the piano

Middle C is in the middle of the Treble and Bass clef staves.

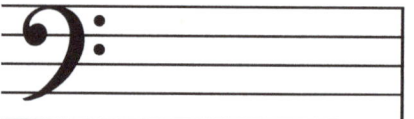
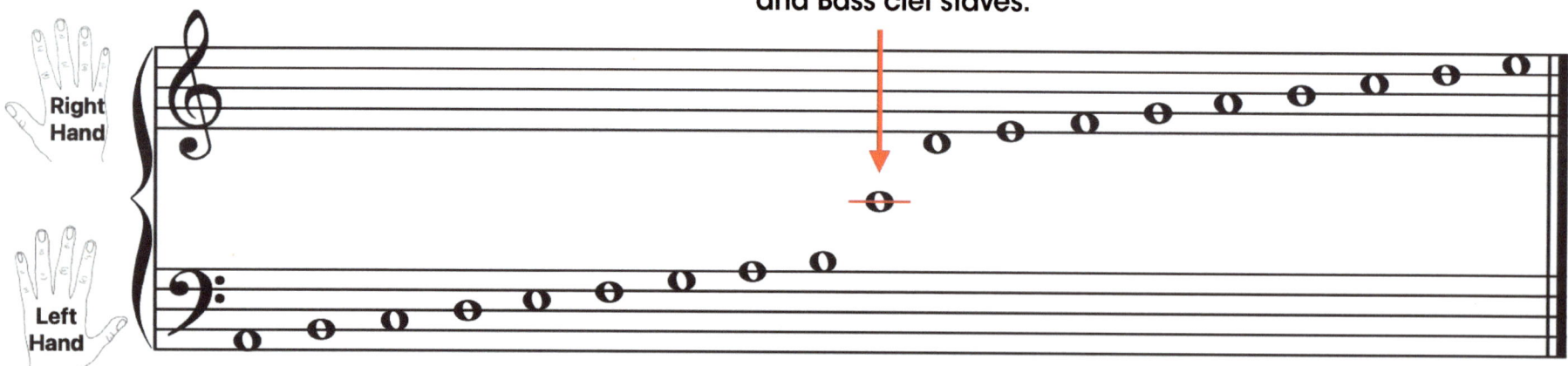

Does Right Hand or Left Hand Play?

In piano music, the right hand notes are written in the top staff
and the left hand notes are written in the bottom staff.
Circle the hand that plays in each circled staff below.

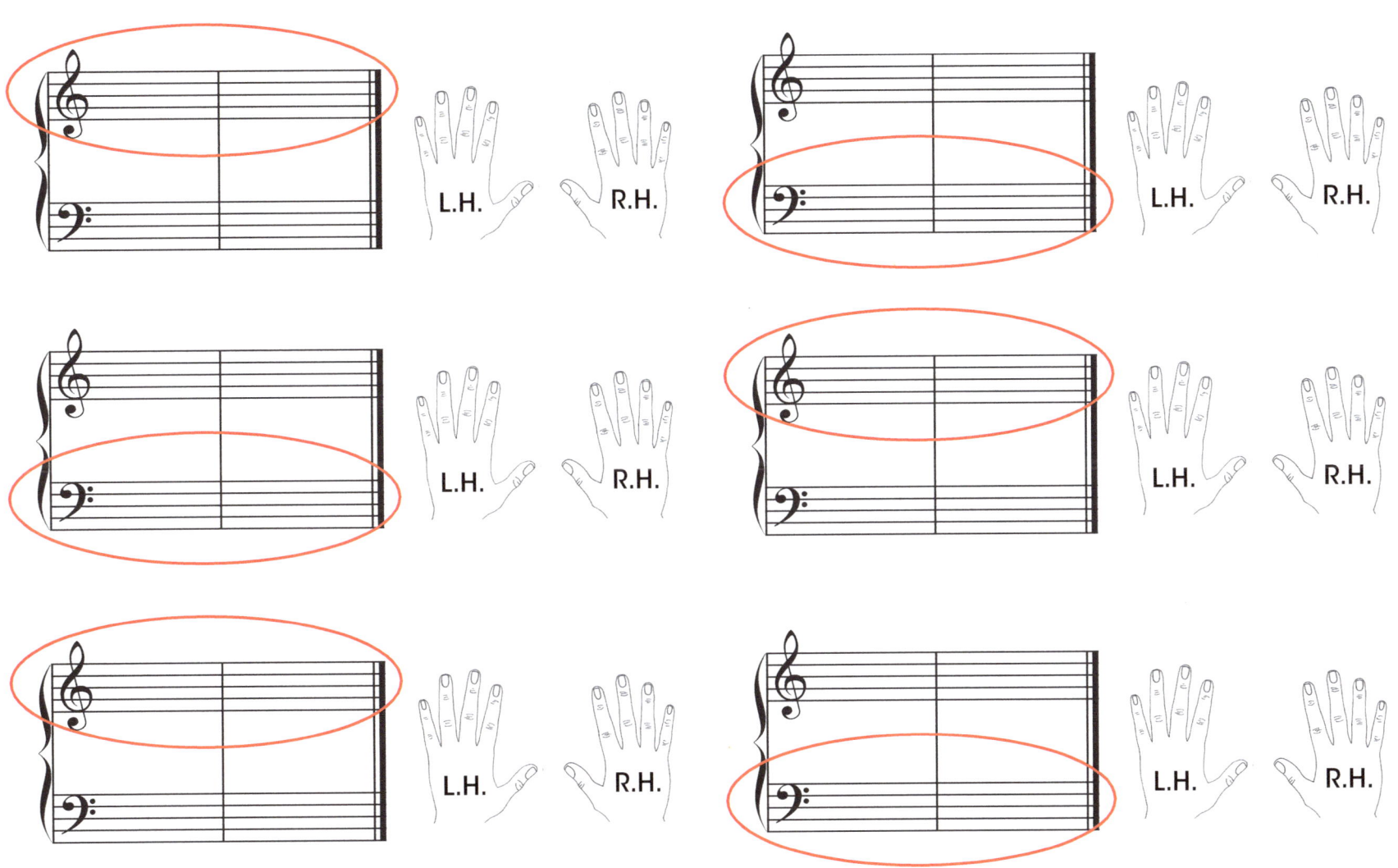

The Rainbow Method Explained

When you read space notes, remember that the entire note head needs to be on the space.

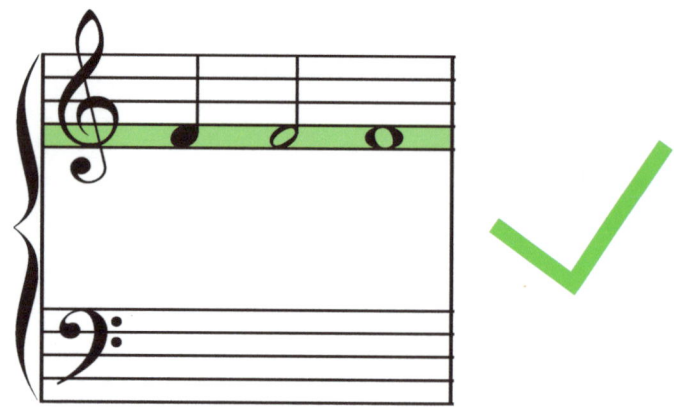

The note head is completely
on the green space.

The note head is only partially on the green space.
This note has a line going through its center,
so it is not on the green space.
It is on the line above the green space.

When you read line notes, remember that the line passes through the center of the note head.

The blue line passes through
the center of the note head, so
this note is on the blue line.

The blue line does not pass through the center of
the note head, so this note is not on the blue line.
This note is on the space below the blue line.

THE NOTES OF THE TREBLE CLEF

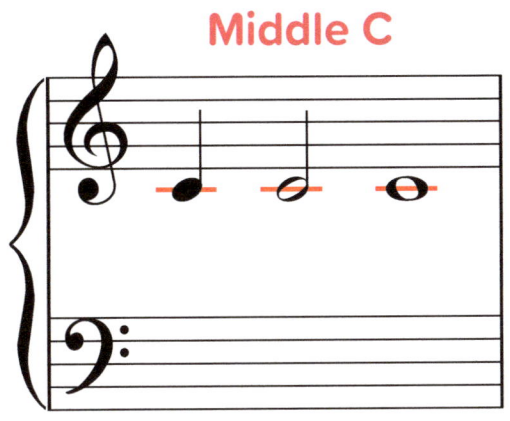

Middle C

Middle C is on the floating line between the treble and bass clef staves.

Look for the notes on the red line.

They all are **Middle C** because they are on the floating red line!

When the right hand plays **Middle C**, the note is written below the treble clef staff.

Middle C
(Right Hand)

f Mid - dle   C   is   ver - y   free!   It   is   a   cool   key!

R.H.

L.H.

Teacher Duet: Student plays 1 octave higher

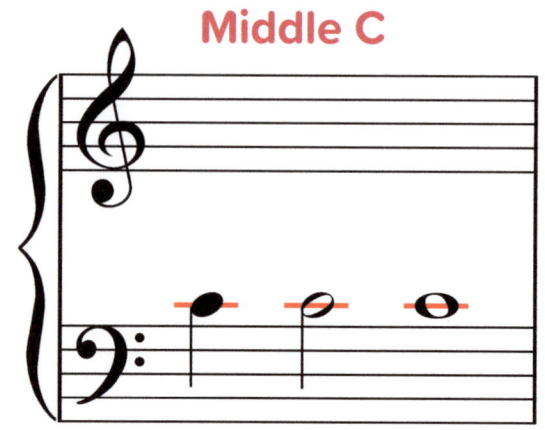

Middle C

Now let's play the whole piece again with the left hand!

When the left hand plays Middle C
the note is written on the same floating red line, but this
time the note is written above the bass clef staff.

Middle C
(Left Hand)

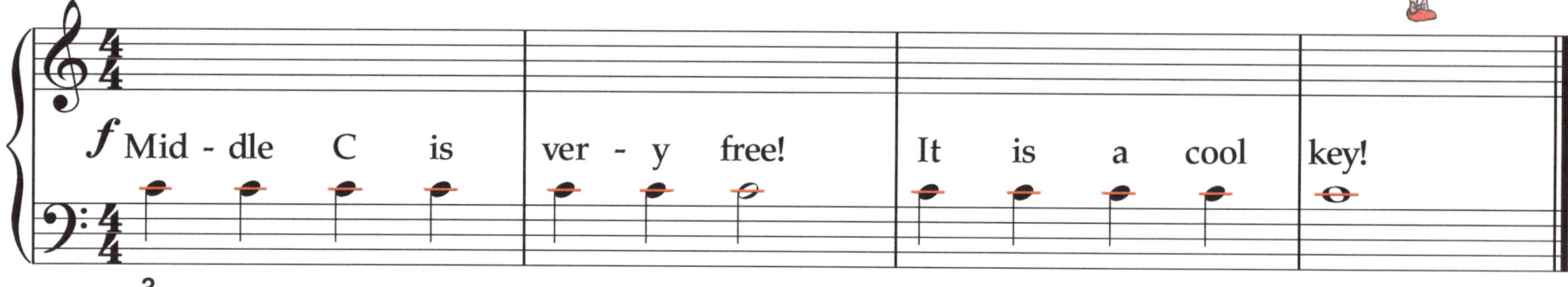

f Mid - dle C is | ver - y free! | It is a cool | key!

3

Teacher Duet: Student plays 1 octave higher

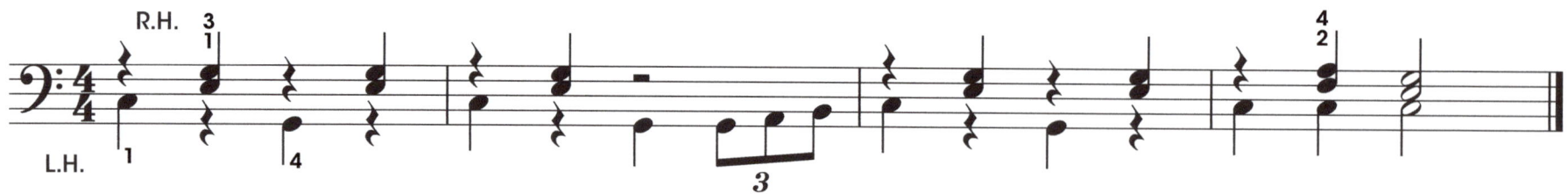

New Time Signature

3 = Count 1 – 2 – 3

4 = ♩ gets 1 beat

3 The top number tells us the number of beats that are in each measure. In this case, there are 3 beats!

4 The bottom number tells us the type of note that gets 1 beat. In this case, quarter notes get 1 beat!

This is one measure

1 2 3   1 2 3   1 2 3

Activity Corner:

1. Can you count and clap the rhythm above?
2. Can you play the notes and count out loud?

Treble D

Treble D is on the space underneath the treble clef staff.

Do you see the orange notes?

They all are Treble D!

C Meets D Waltz

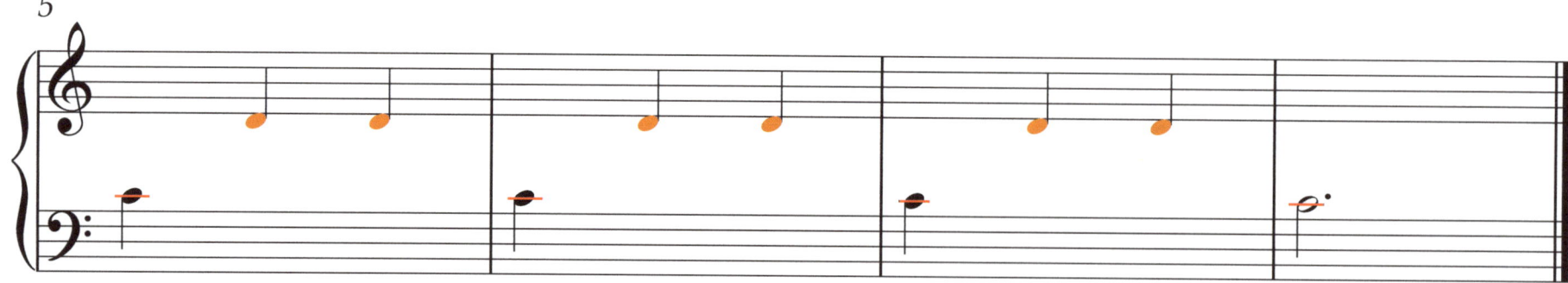

Seconds

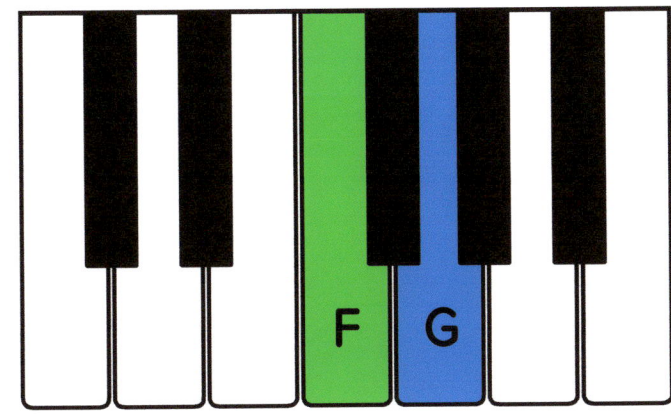

Seconds (Steps)

Seconds are notes that are next to each other on the piano and the staff.

Seconds move from a space to the next line or a line to the next space on the staff.

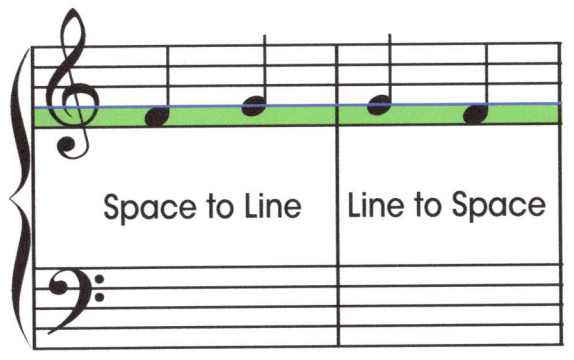

When we read music it is important to think about HOW the notes are moving on the staff. Are the notes stepping up or down?

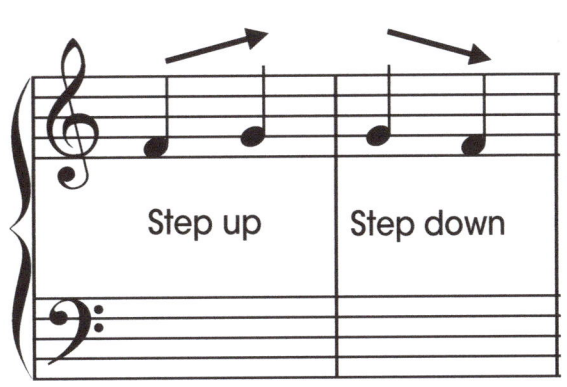

Activity Corner: Are the notes in the measures below stepping up or stepping down? Circle the correct answer in each box.

Splashing in the Puddle

Hold the pedal down for the entire piece.

Do you see the pedal marking below?

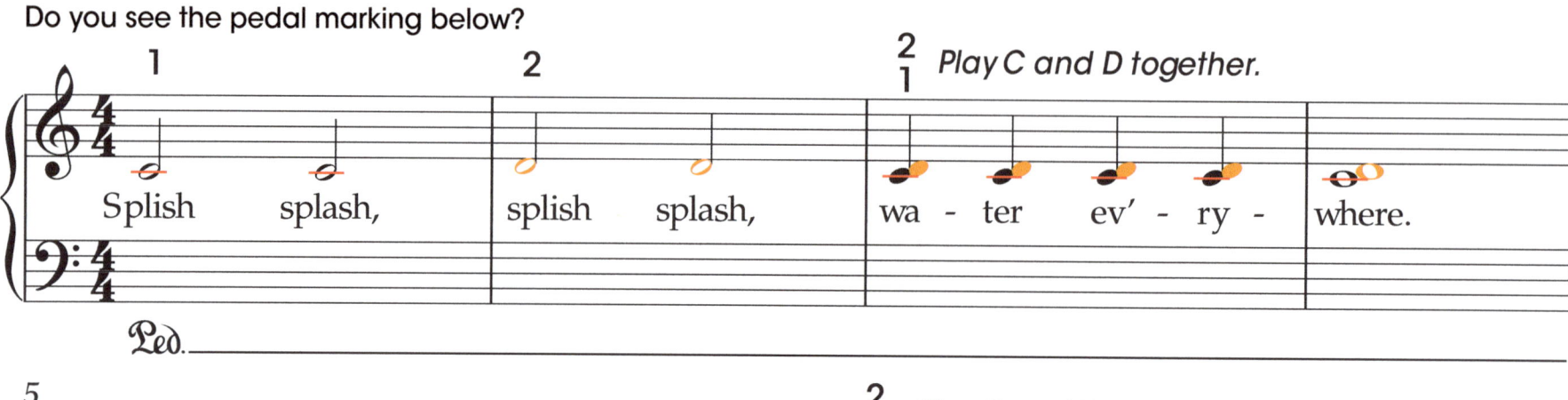

Splish   splash,   splish   splash,   wa - ter   ev' - ry -   where.

Play C and D together.

Ped.

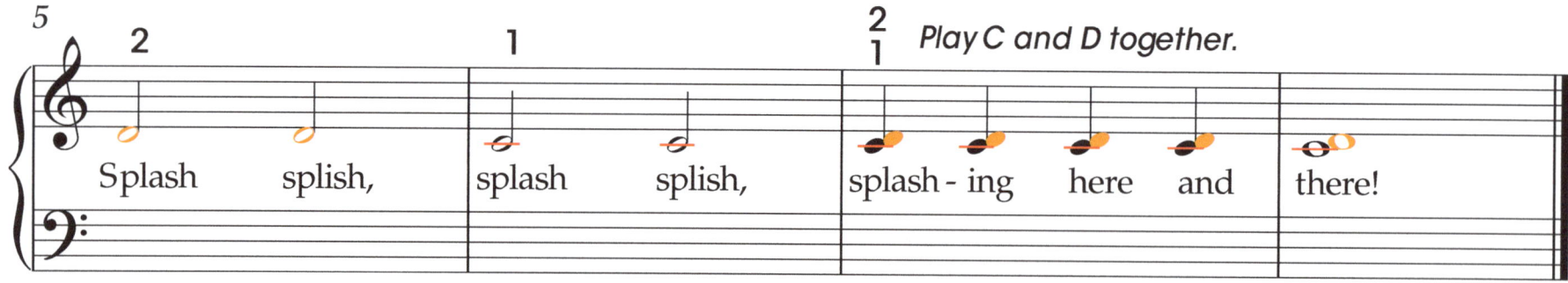

Splash   splish,   splash   splish,   splash - ing   here   and   there!

Play C and D together.

Treble E

Treble E is on the bottom line of the treble clef staff.

Do you see the notes on the yellow line? They all are Treble E!

Elephants, Donkeys, and Crocodiles

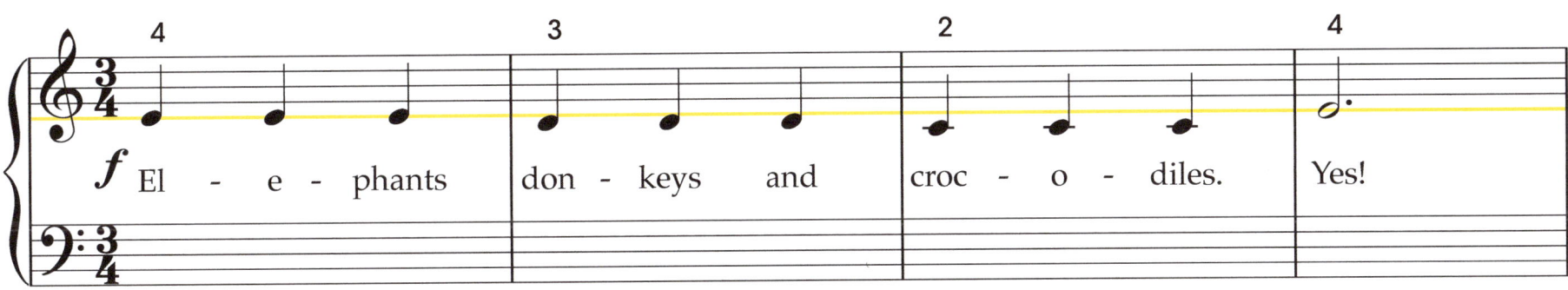

f El - e - phants | don - keys and | croc - o - diles. | Yes!

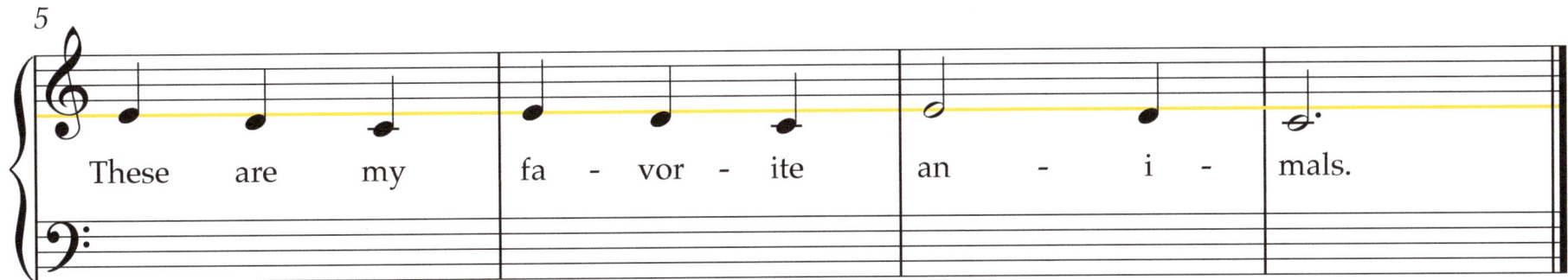

These are my | fa - vor - ite | an - i - | mals.

39

Activity Corner:

Fill in the names of the notes in the blanks below.

Mary Had a Little Lamb

Traditional

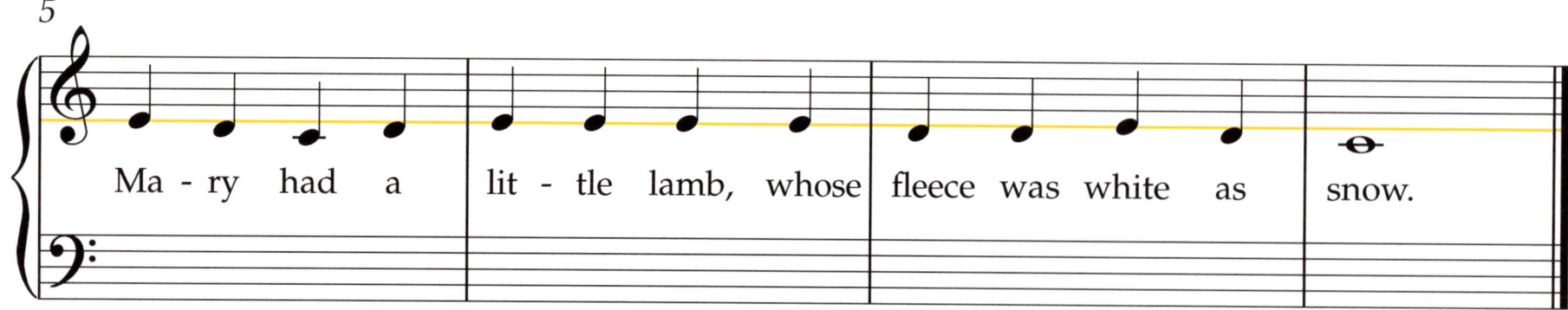

Treble F is on the first space of the treble clef staff.

Do you see the notes on the green space?

They all are Treble F!

Treble F
(To the tune of "Baby Shark")

Traditional
Arr. Ariel Nathnson Bolinja

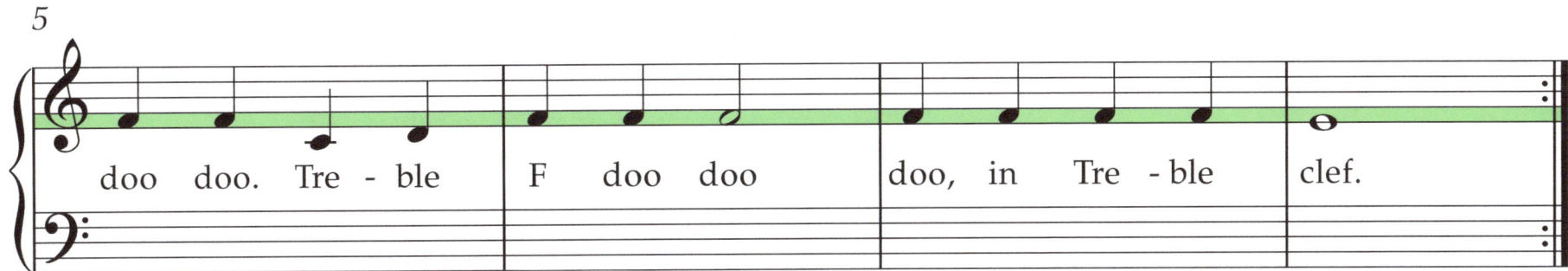

41

Activity Corner:

How many Treble F's can you count in this piece?

Write your answer below:

I Can Read EF!

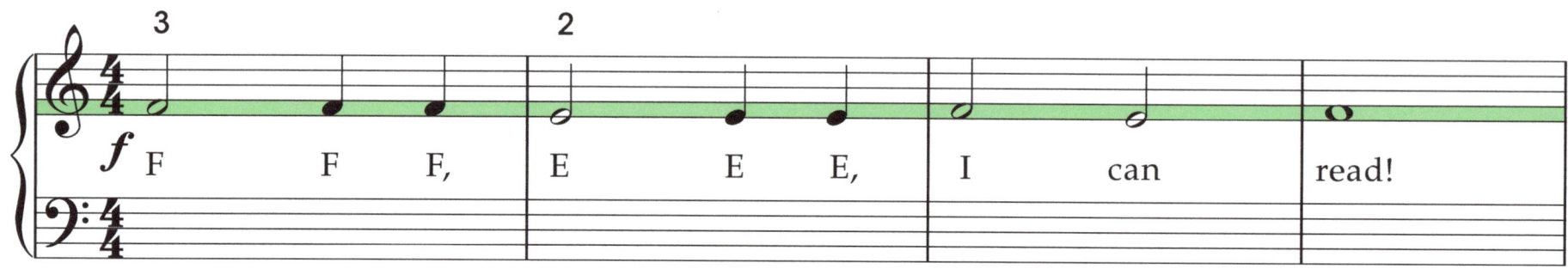

F F F, E E E, I can read!

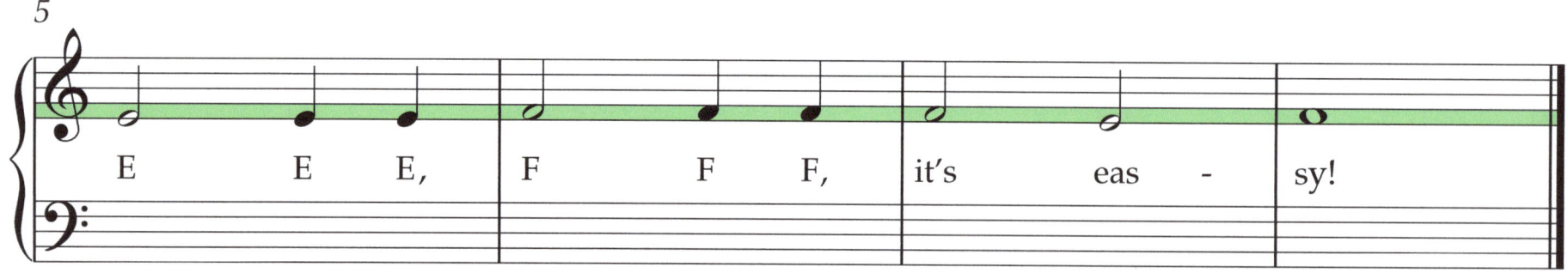

E E E, F F F, it's eas - sy!

Treble G

Treble G is on the second line of the treble clef staff.

The treble clef symbol circles the Treble G line.

Do you see the notes on the blue line?

They all are Treble G!

Should this piece be played f or p?

Write in the dynamic sign in the box below.

Treble G

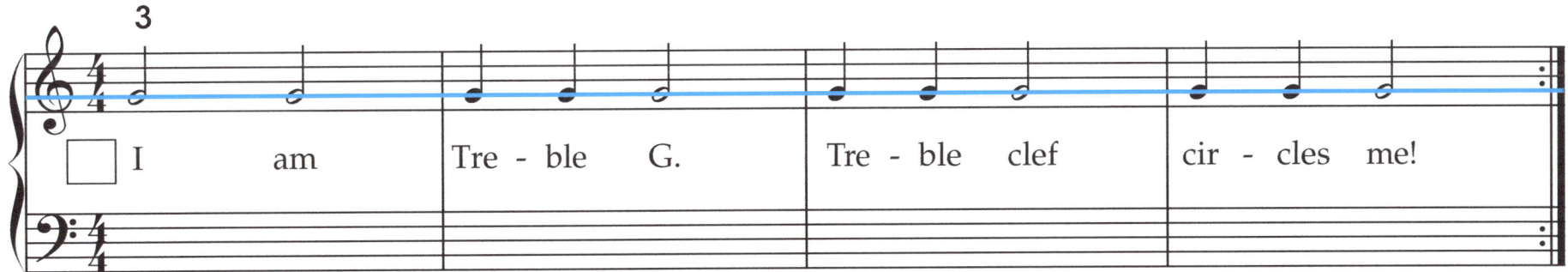

I am Tre - ble G. Tre - ble clef cir - cles me!

Teacher Duet: Student plays 1 octave higher

43

Jingle Bells

Traditional

mf Jin - gle bells,   jin - gle bells,   jin - gle   all   the   way.

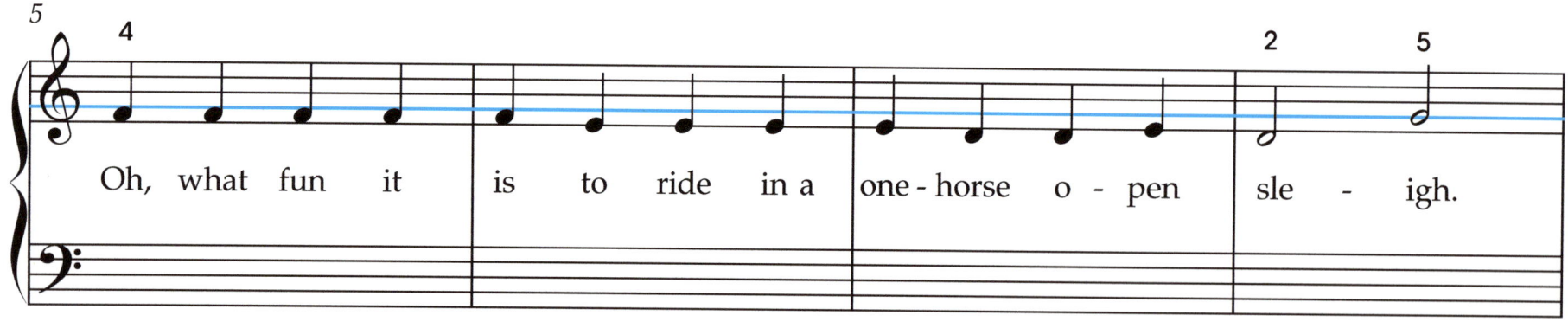

Oh, what fun it   is to ride in a   one - horse o - pen   sle - igh.

Jin - gle bells, jin - gle bells, jin - gle all the way.

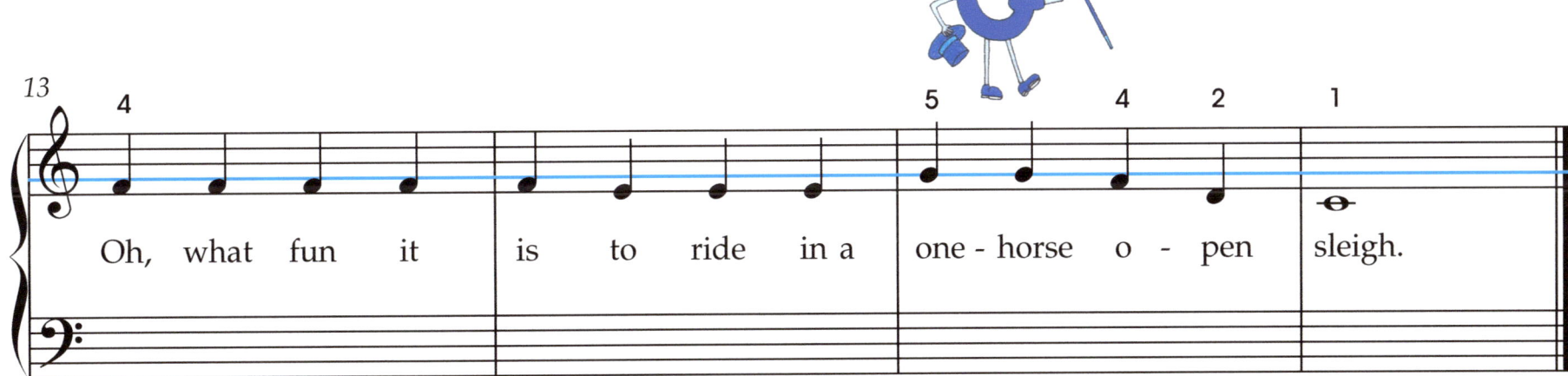

Oh, what fun it is to ride in a one - horse o - pen sleigh.

Treble Clef Note Review

Write the names of the notes in the blanks below.

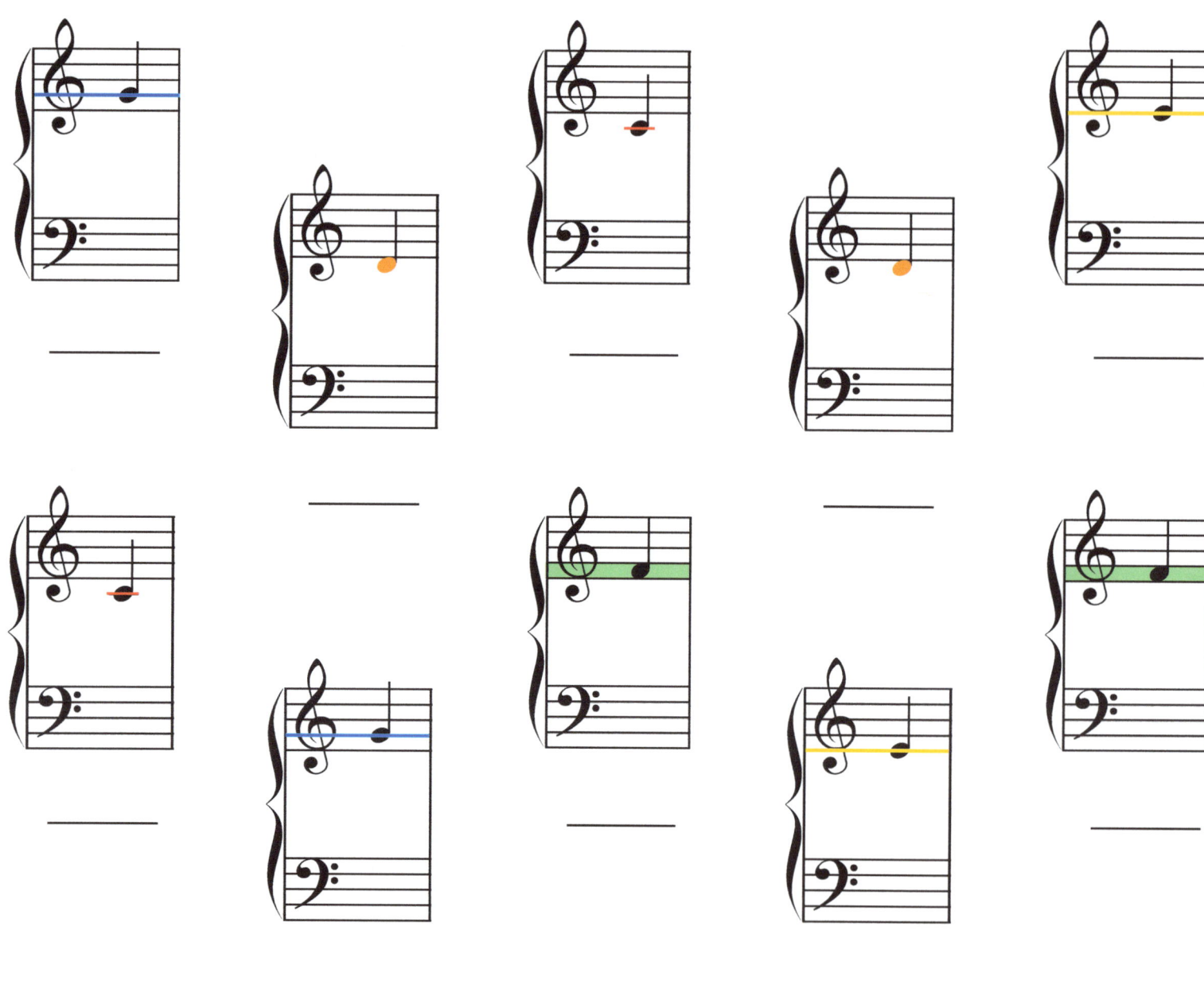

Treble Clef Note Review

Write the names of the notes in the blanks below.

THE NOTES OF THE BASS CLEF

Bass B

Bass B is on the space above the Bass Clef staff.

Do you see the pink note? That is **Bass B**!

My Pet Cat

mf My pet cat, his name's Tom. His black fur is quite long.

Loves to sleep in the sun. Plays with toys pranc - ing a - long.

R.H. 4 1

mp
L.H. 3

Teacher Duet: Student plays 1 octave higher

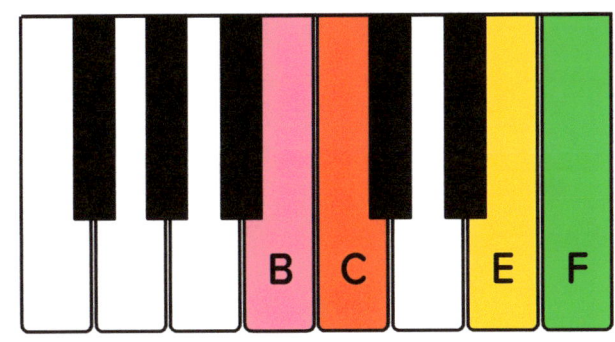

Half Steps

Half Steps are the smallest step on the piano. Two notes that are right next to each other with no note in between.

Look at E and F. Do you see how there is no black key in between them? That is a half step!

Haunted Half Steps

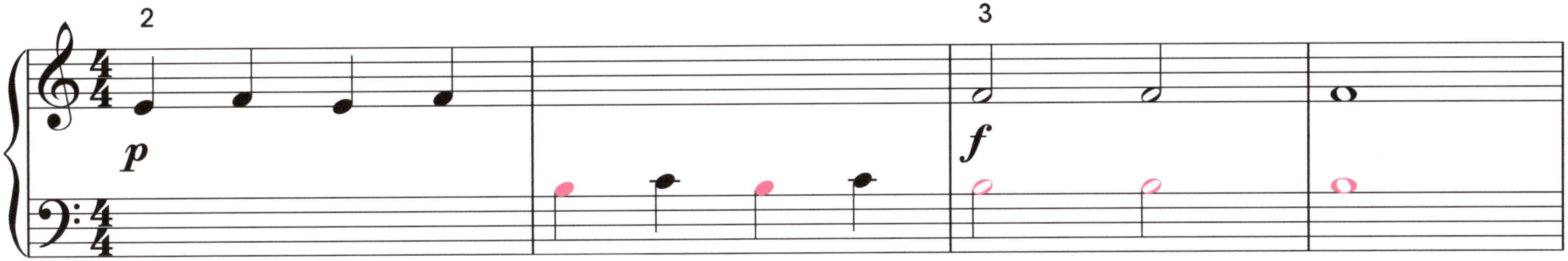

Teacher Duet: Student plays 1 octave higher

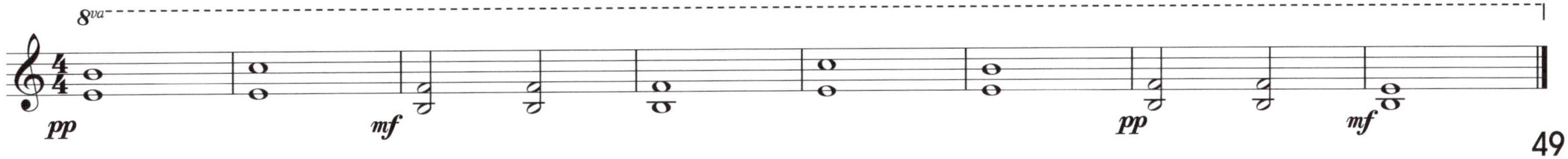

(Play the second lowest E on the piano)

Bass A

Bass A is on the top line of the bass clef staff.

Do you see the notes on the purple line?

They all are **Bass A**!

Halloween Monster

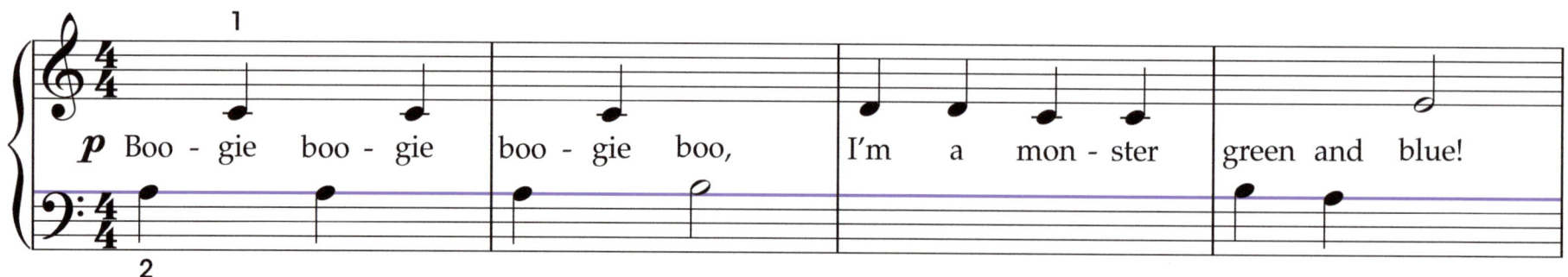

p Boo - gie boo - gie boo - gie boo, I'm a mon - ster green and blue!

f Boo - gie boo - gie boo - gie boo, scar - ing you is what I do!

Teacher Duet: Student plays 1 octave higher

The Dynamics Zoo

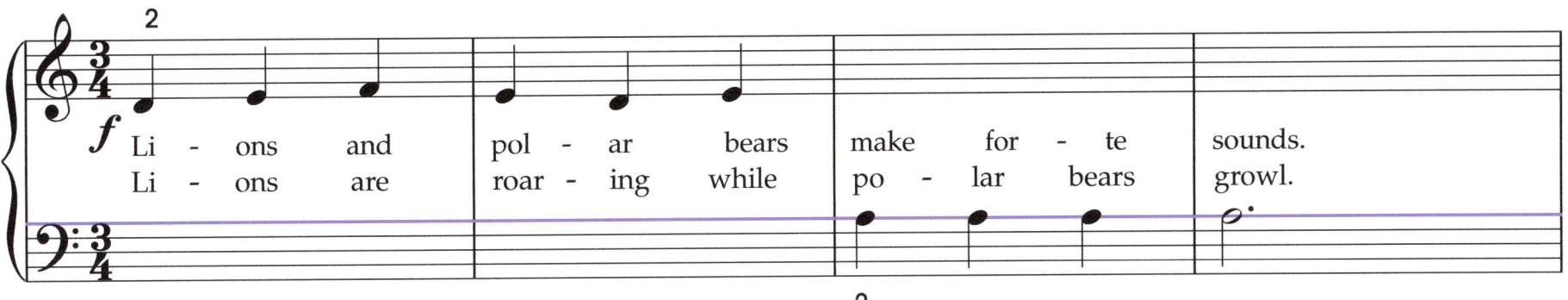

Li - ons and pol - ar bears make for - te sounds.
Li - ons are roar - ing bears while po - lar bears growl.

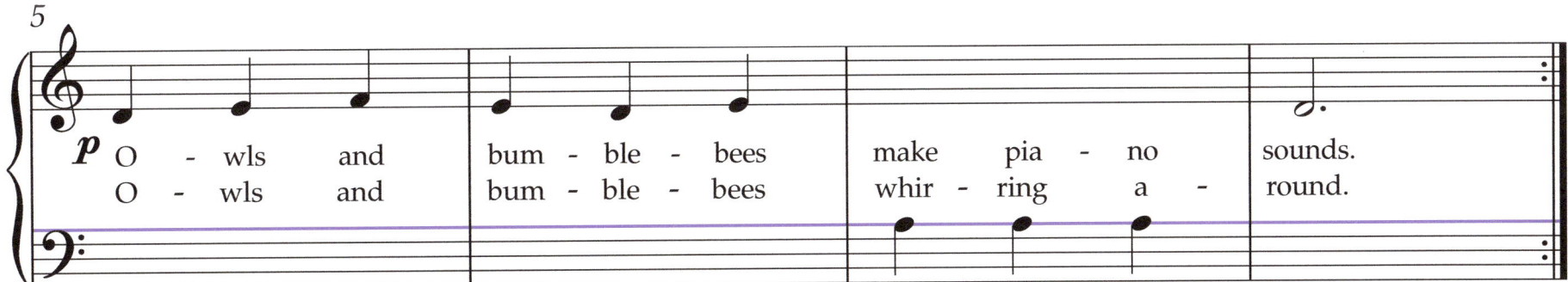

O - wls and bum - ble - bees make pia - no sounds.
O - wls and bum - ble - bees whir - ring a - round.

How many Bass A's can you count in this piece?

Thirds

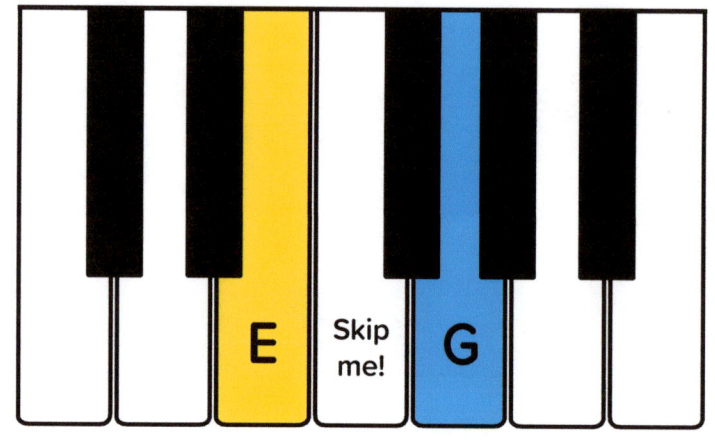

Thirds (Skips)

Thirds are two notes that are separated by one letter in the musical alphabet. Skip over a note on the keyboard to get to the next note.

Thirds move from a line to the next line or a space to the next space on the staff. Skip over a line or space to get to the next note!

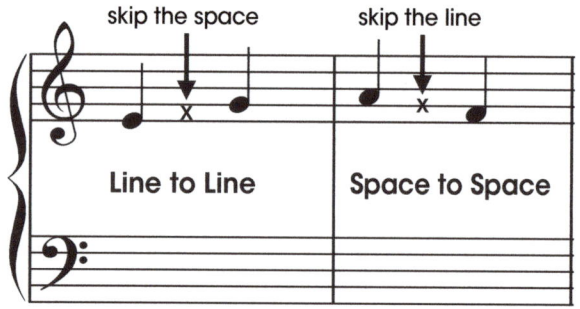

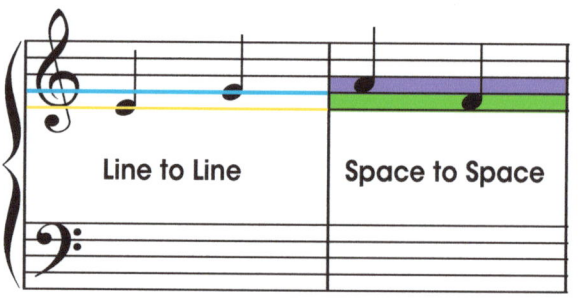

Activity Corner: Are the notes in the measures below stepping or skipping? Circle the correct answer in each box.

Stepping, Skipping

Step - ping, skip - ping, on the keys. Skip - ping, step - ping with great ease.

Step - ping, skip - ping is so fun. Skip - ping, step - ping now we're done!

Teacher Duet: Student plays 1 octave higher

Bass G

Bass G is on the top space of the bass clef staff.

Do you see the notes on the blue space?

They all are Bass G!

Summer Day

54

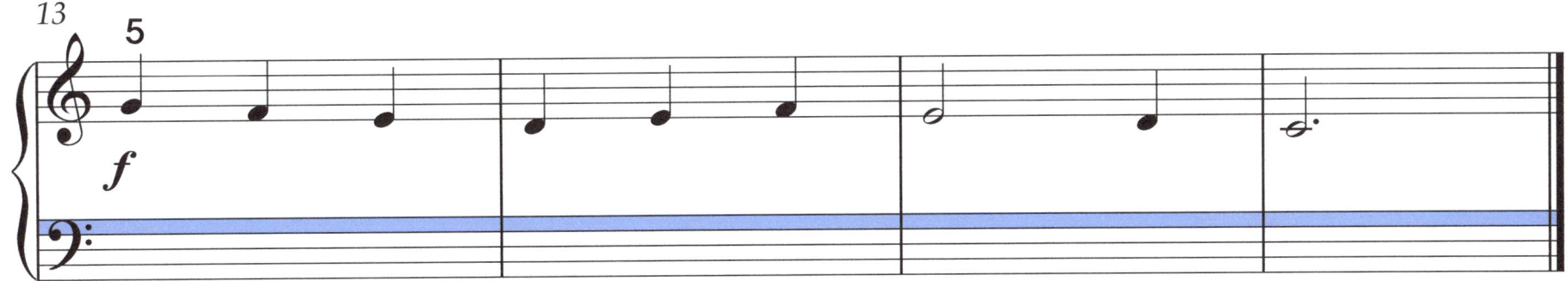

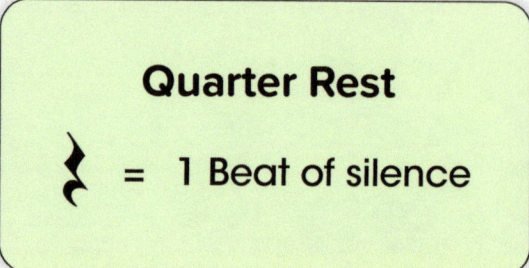

Quarter Rest

𝄽 = 1 Beat of silence

Activity Corner:

Draw 2 quarter rests in the space below!

Before you play:

1. Write the counts out in the rainbow spaces below.

2. Practice counting and clapping the rhythm.
   Clap on the quarter notes. Do not clap on the rests.

I Like to Rest!

mf I   like to rest, rest, rest, rest! Play-ing's fun but rest-ing is the best!

Bass F

Bass F is on the 4th line of the bass clef staff.

The Bass F line passes between the two dots of the bass clef symbol.

Do you see the notes on the green line?

They all are **Bass F**!

Bass F

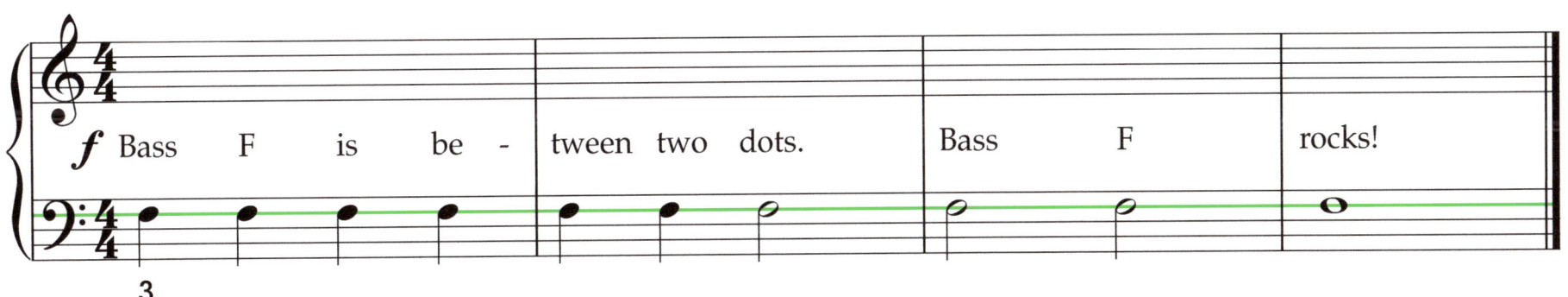

f Bass   F   is   be - tween two dots.   Bass   F   rocks!

3

Teacher Duet: Student plays as written

Ties

Ties connect two notes together to create one note that equals the number of beats of both notes combined.

Inchworm

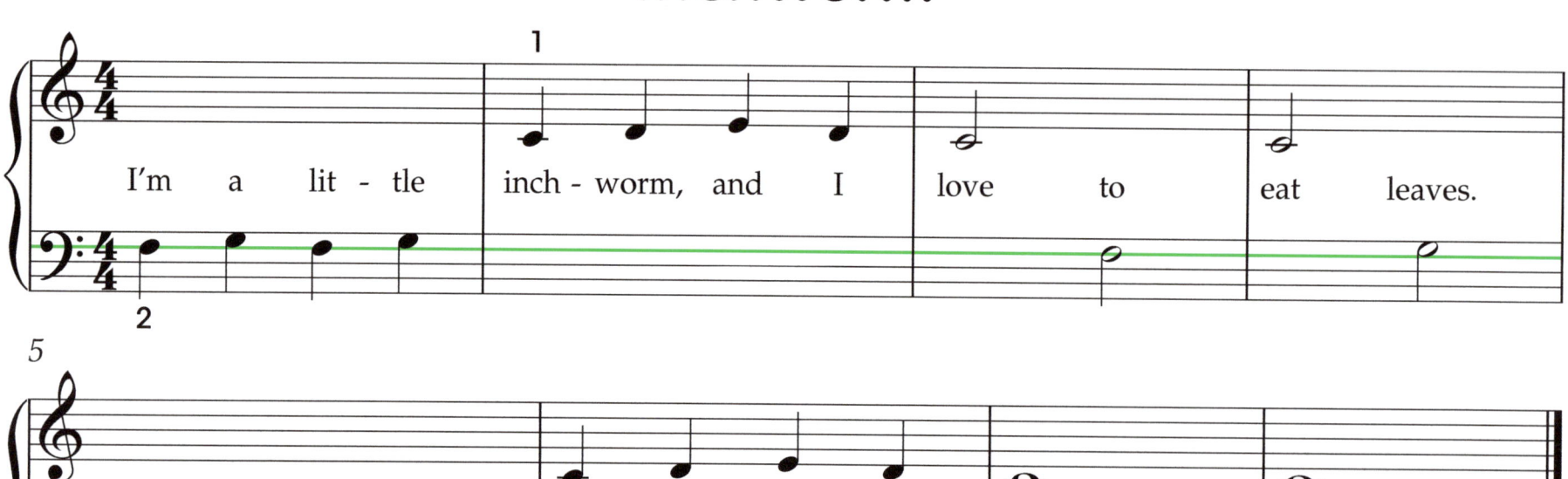

Bass E is on the third space of the bass clef.

Do you see the notes on the yellow space?

They all are **Bass E**!

Fermata

Hold the note for longer than its usual value.

You can decide how long to hold it!

Beethoven's Fifth Symphony Theme

Ludwig van Beethoven (1770-1827)
Arr. Ariel Nathanson Bolinja

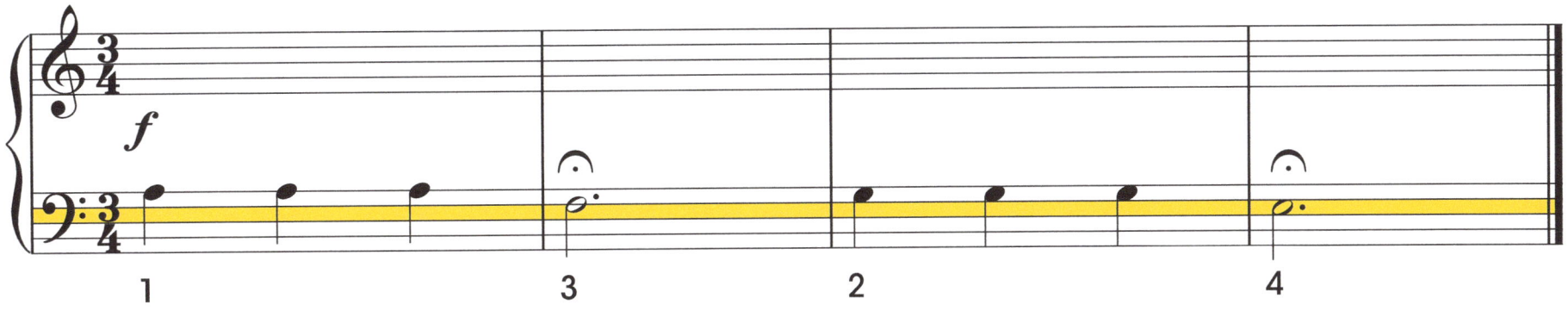

Bass D

Bass D is on the third line of the bass clef staff.

Do you see the notes on the orange line?

They all are Bass D!

Snakes

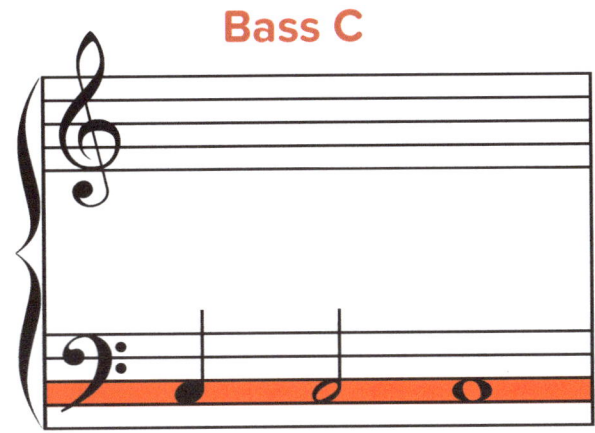

Bass C

Bass C is on the second space of the bass clef.

Do you see the notes on the red space?

They all are Bass C!

Can you find all of the Bass C's?

C Major Five-Finger Scale

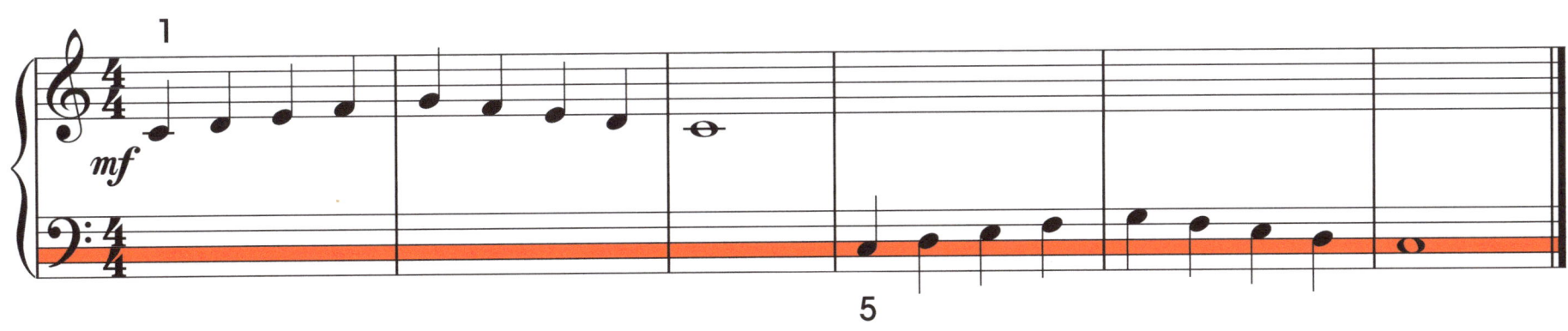

61

Bass Clef Note Review

Write the names of the notes in the blanks below.

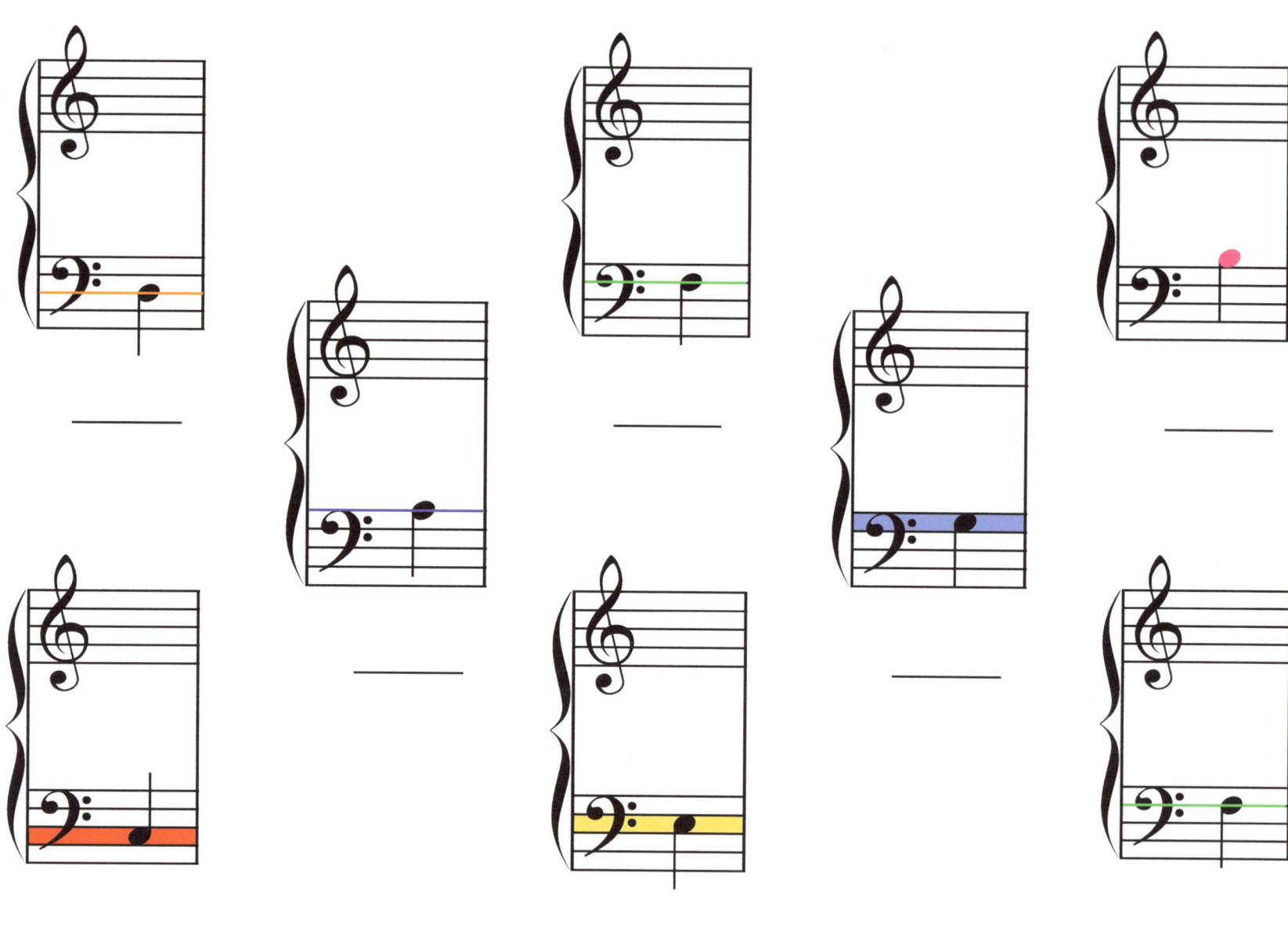

Bass Clef Note Review

Write the names of the notes in the blanks below.

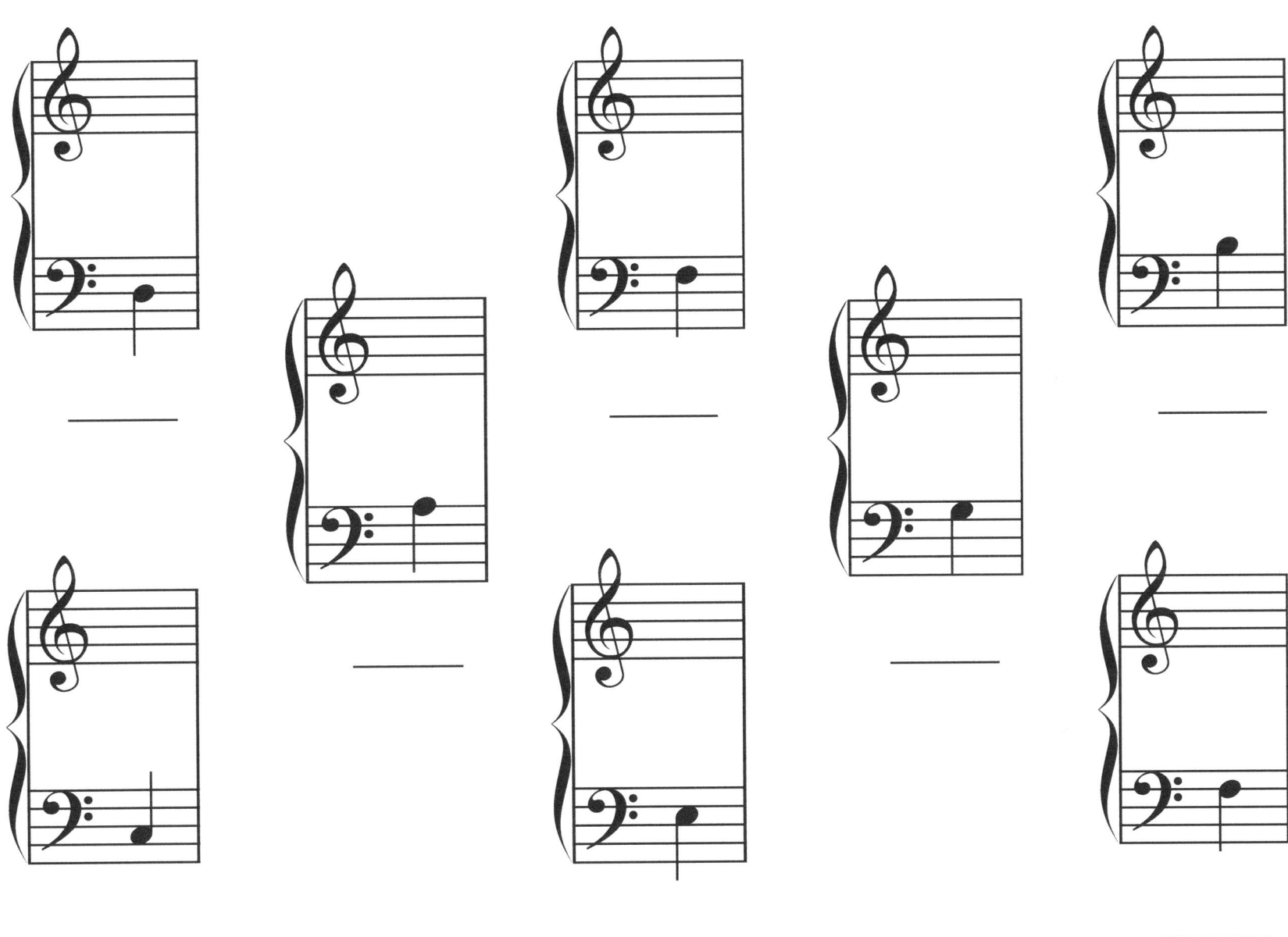

Sight-Reading Fun!

What is Sight-Reading?

Musicians sight-read when they play a piece for the first time by reading the notes from their musical score.

Now it is your turn to sight-read! Before you play each exercise, follow these instructions:

1. Count and clap the rhythm.
2. Look at how the notes move:
   - Do they step or skip?
   - Do they move higher or lower?

Move your finger along with the notes to follow the direction in which they move.

3. Look at the starting notes and finger numbers.
4. Now, play the exercise and make sure to count!

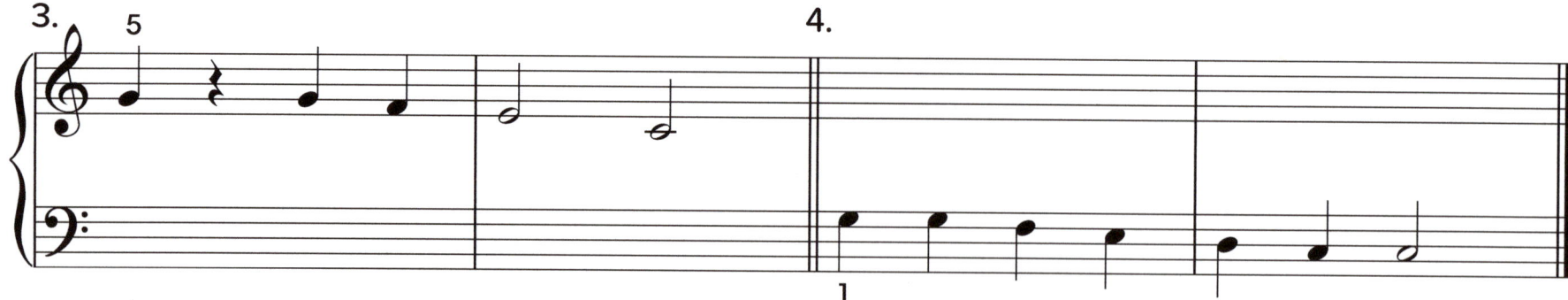

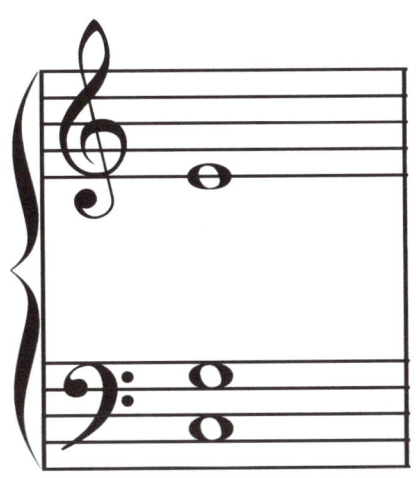

Playing notes together:

When notes are written on top of each other they are played together at the same time.

In this piece, left hand plays two notes at the same time!

Did you know?

The first organ was water-powered and invented in ancient Greece. Now, organs produce their sound with pressurized air that is pushed through pipes when you depress each key.

The Organ Player

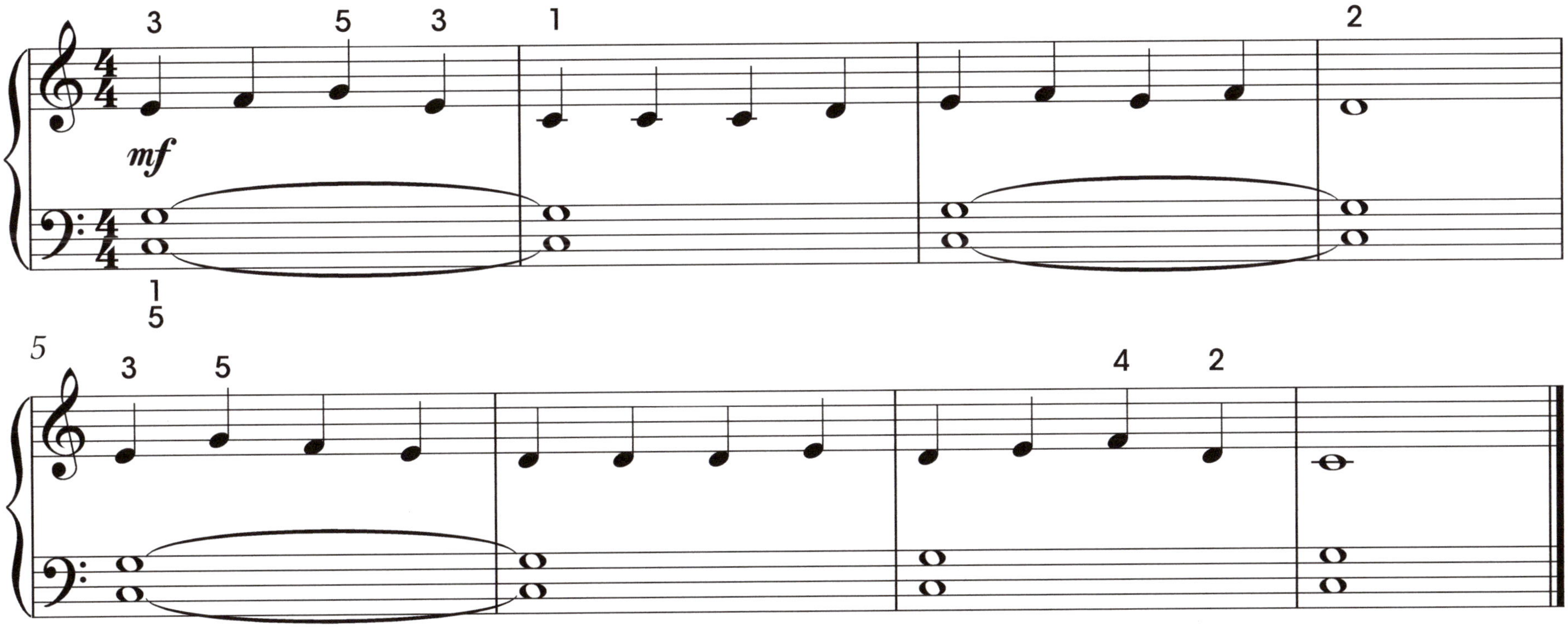

Practice tip: Practice hands separately first!

1 2 3 4 5

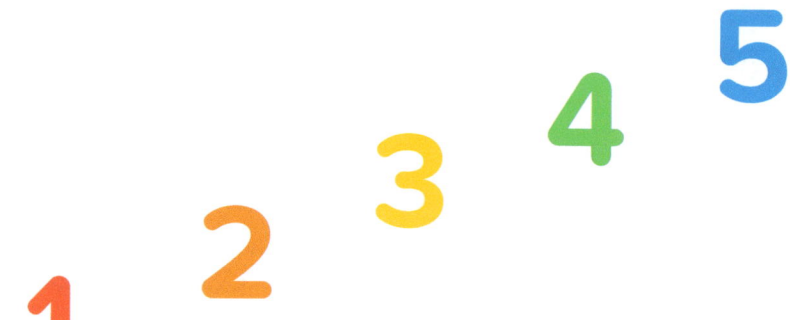

Activity Corner:

Count all of the thirds (skips) in this piece and write how many you found here:

____

The Five-Note March

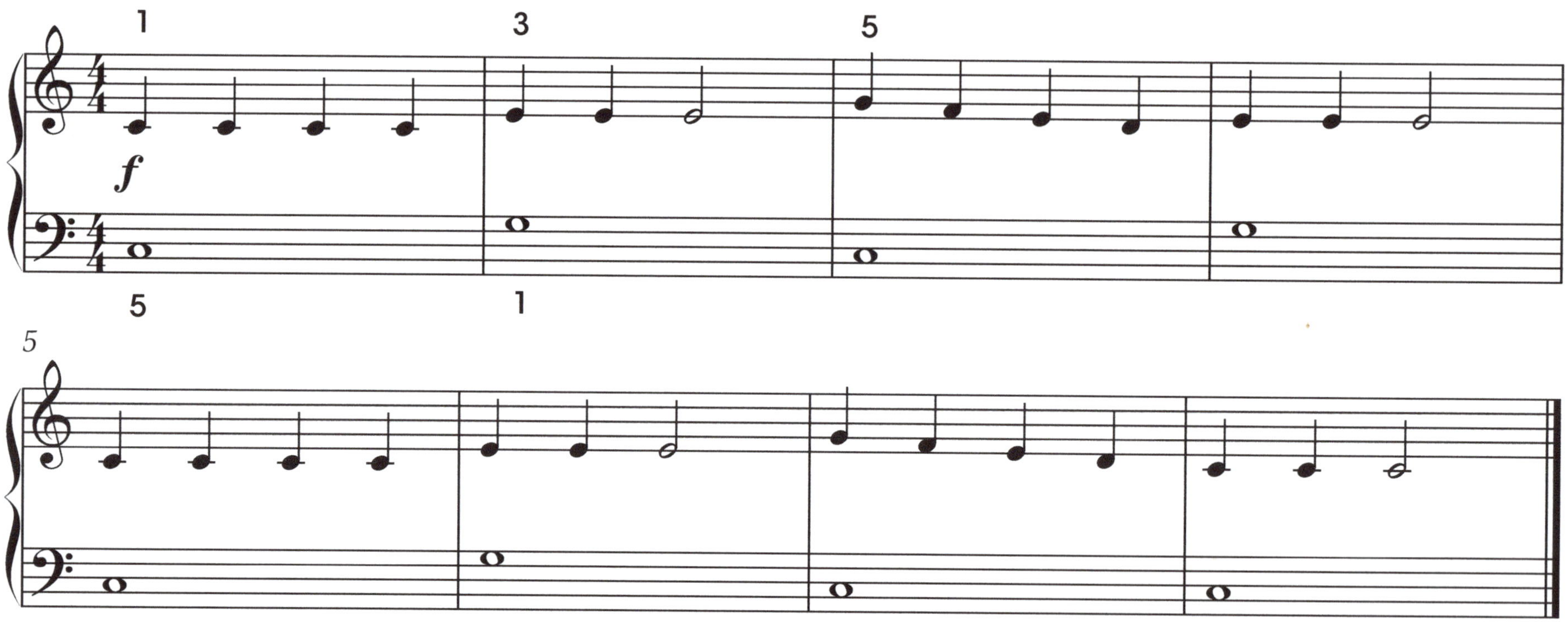

Practice tip: Practice hands separately first!

SHARPS AND FLATS · TREBLE A AND B

Treble A

Treble A is on the second space of the treble clef staff.

Do you see the notes on the purple space?

They all are **Treble A**!

Can you find all of the Treble A's?

In the Valley

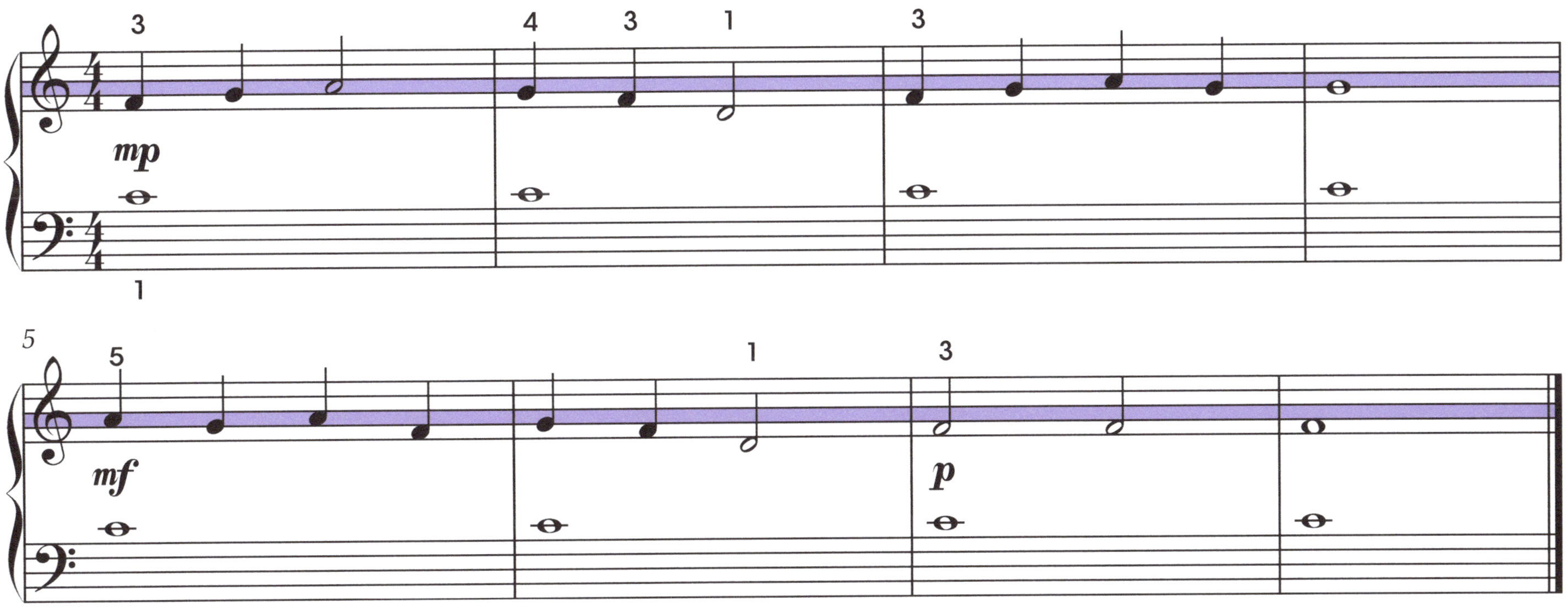

Flats

♭ This is the flat symbol. It tells you to play the note a half step lower.

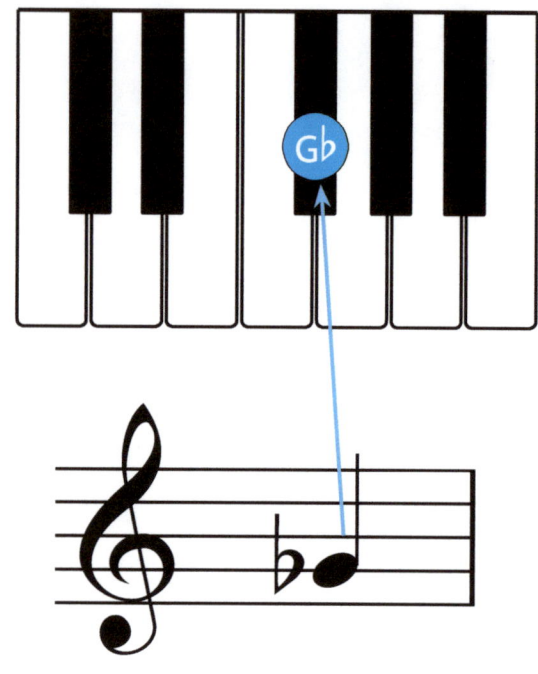

This note is G♭

Do you see the blue arrow pointing to the G♭ on the keyboard?

This note is _____

Now draw an arrow pointing to the correct flat on the keyboard.

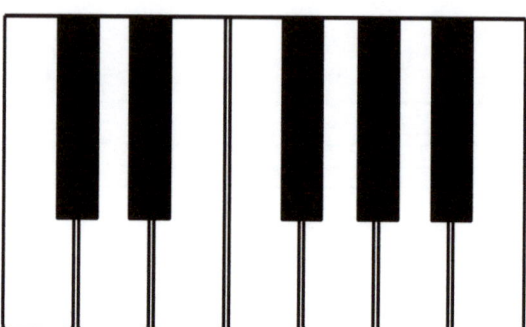

This note is _____

Now draw an arrow pointing to the correct flat on the keyboard.

Activity Corner:

What note is flat in this piece?

Write your answer in the space below.

Dragon's Lair

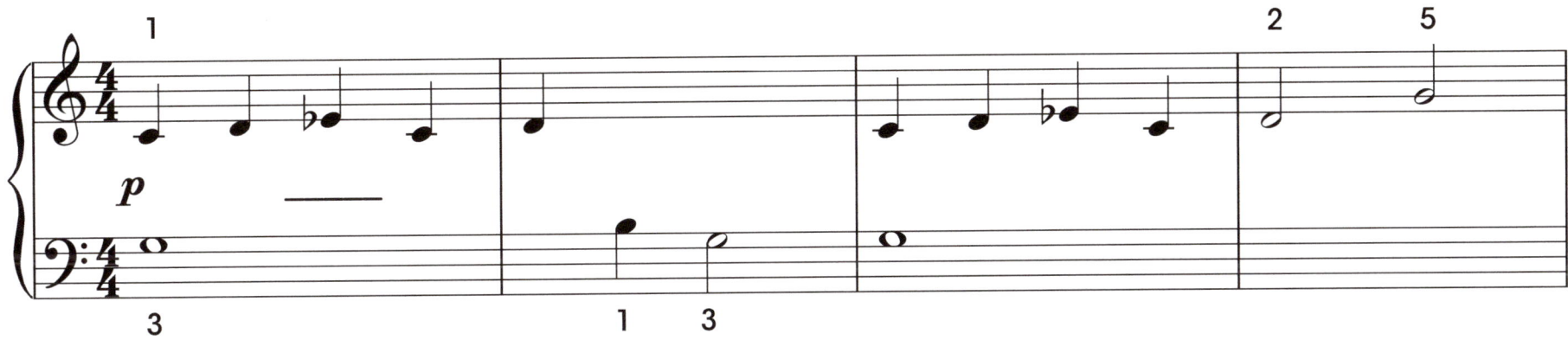

Sharps

 This is the sharp symbol. It tells you to play the note a half step higher.

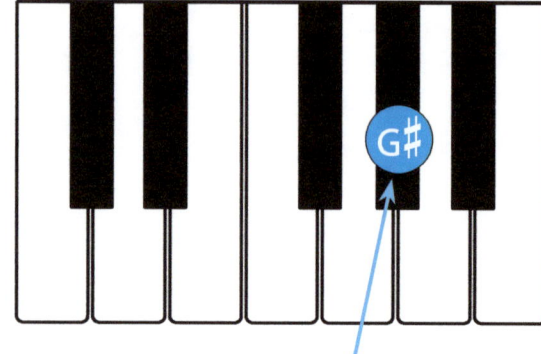

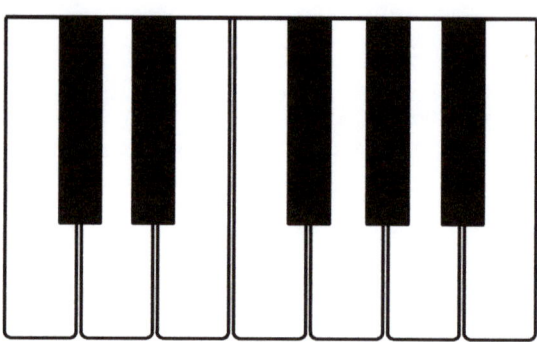

This note is G♯

Do you see the blue arrow pointing to the G♯ on the keyboard?

This note is _____

Now draw an arrow pointing to the correct sharp on the keyboard.

This note is _____

Now draw an arrow pointing to the correct sharp on the keyboard.

Treble B

Treble B is on the third line of the treble clef staff.

Do you see the notes on the pink line?

They all are Treble B!

What note is sharp in this piece?

Gray Sky

Activity Corner:

What notes are sharp in this piece? Write the names of the sharp notes in the rainbow spaces below.

Starry Night

Hold the damper pedal down throughout the entire piece.

LH over - Your teacher will demonstrate how to play these notes (C♯ and D♯).

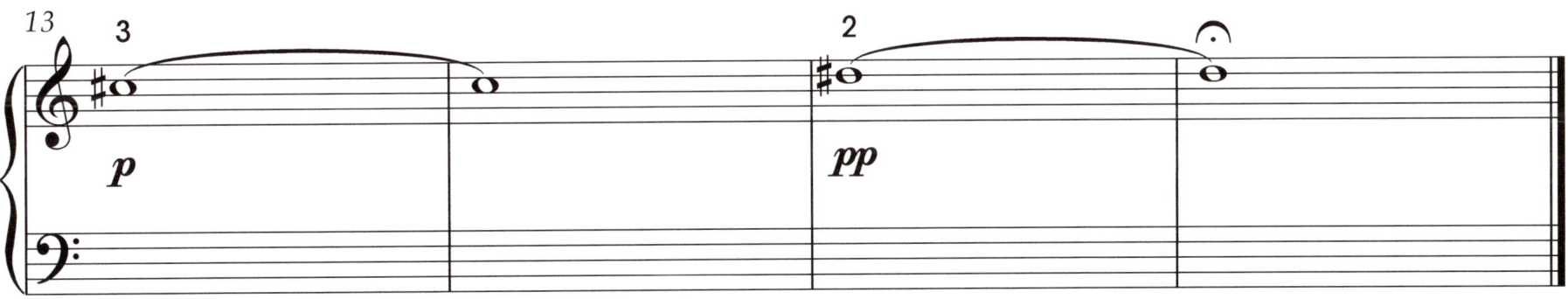

GRADUATION

Did You Know?

A minuet is a dance for two people in 3/4 time. The minuet was a popular European dance during the late 17th century through the 18th century.

Miniature Minuet

Congratulations

_____

Name

You completed the primer level book of
The Rainbow Method!

Now, you are ready for:
The Rainbow Method Level 1

_____   _____

Teacher Signature   Date